Solitude

Solitude

In Pursuit of a Singular Life in a Crowded World

Michael Harris

BOOKS

1 3 5 7 9 10 8 6 4 2

Random House Books
20 Vauxhall Bridge Road
London SW1V 2SA

Random House Books is part of the Penguin Random House group of companies
whose addresses can be found at global.penguinrandomhouse.com.

First published by Random House Books in 2017

www.penguin.co.uk

A CIP catalogue record for this book is available from the British Library.

ISBN 9781847947642 (hardback)
ISBN 9781847947659 (trade paperback)

For David Anderson and Kenny Park

Contents

There is another Loneliness

—Emily Dickinson

Foreword

Every life has a rhythm. For most creatures on the planet, that rhythm reflects an ongoing negotiation between the body and its surroundings, between being and environment. There's a time for resting, a time for hunting, a time for courting, a time for hiding. For us humans, though, it's more complicated than that. Because we have the power to shape our environment, through laws and customs, economic and political systems, and, not least, technologies, we are also able to control the rhythm of our lives.

That, it turns out, is a mixed blessing. On the one hand, it frees us from the grip of necessity. We're able to make choices about how we spend our time. On the other hand, we can, and frequently do, fall into a daily rhythm that ill suits us or runs counter to our best interests. We fill our days with activities that provide fleeting pleasures or momentary conveniences but that leave us feeling anxious or unfulfilled. In the worst cases, we surrender control over the rhythm of our life to others—to bosses or bureaucrats, to marketers or technicians. We end up living according to a rhythm imposed on us rather than one chosen by us. We dance to someone else's drum.

In this wise and witty book, Michael Harris examines a phenomenon that is altering the rhythm of human life in profound and unsettling ways: the loss of solitude. For more than a century, human life has been getting busier and busier. Media bombard us with messages and diversions. Work time bleeds into leisure time. The social whirl spins ever faster. Until recently, though, there were still moments in the day when the busyness abated and life's pace decelerated. You would find yourself alone, separated from friends and colleagues, and you would be thrown back on your own resources, your own thoughts. Such interludes could provoke feelings of loneliness and boredom. Yet they also provided opportunities to tap into ideas, perceptions, and emotions inaccessible to the social self.

Now, those moments are being erased. With smartphone in hand, connectivity is continuous. We're in a crowd even when we're by ourselves. The chatter never ends; the rhythm never slows. Nonstop networking may feel invigorating, but, as Harris makes clear, we sacrifice much when we're never alone. Solitude is refreshing. It strengthens memory, sharpens awareness, and spurs creativity. It makes us calmer, more attentive, clearer headed. Most important of all, it relieves the pressure of conformity. It gives us the space we need to discover the deepest sources of passion, enjoyment, and fulfillment in our lives. Being alone frees us to be ourselves—and that makes us better company when we rejoin the crowd.

The art of solitude—the art that, as Harris elegantly puts it, turns "blank days into blank canvases"—is hard to master and easy to squander. Contemporary forces of technology, society, and commerce, beneficial forces in so many ways, conspire not only to diminish our opportunities for solitude but to seduce us into believing that solitude is at best inessential and at worst a waste of time. We should resist those forces. We should remind ourselves that a life without solitude is a diminished life. What makes this book so valuable and so timely is that it serves both as a reminder of solitude's worth and as a spur to resistance. Read it in peace.

Nicholas Carr, author of several acclaimed books on technology and culture, including *Utopia Is Creepy*, *The Glass Cage*, and the Pulitzer Prize–finalist *The Shallows*.

The Dark-Born Magic

Dr. Edith Bone has decided not to cry.

On this autumn afternoon in 1956, her seven years of solitary confinement have come to a sudden end. Beyond the prison gates, the Hungarian Revolution's final, scattered shots are echoing down the streets of Budapest. Inside the gates, Dr. Bone emerges through the prison's front door into the courtyard's bewildering sunlight. She is sixty-eight years old, stout and arthritic. She steps from the prison's entrance and blinks at the sky. And then she sees them waiting for her. Those suited, peering men. They are all waiting to see her tears.

Photographers and reporters hoist their barrel lenses and spiral notebooks by the gleaming bus that has come to take her to the British embassy. They watch for the mark of those seven years alone. What scar does such isolation leave on the face? On the hooded eyes? The ordinary result is a descent into madness and crippling depression. But as Dr. Bone steps slowly across the courtyard toward the iron gates, she appears perfectly sane. If anything, she now looks cheerful. The officials and journalists stare. A man from England's *Daily Express* scribbles in his notebook, trying his best to dramatize things: he writes that she is limping. Later, in a week or so, he'll be embarrassed to learn she was simply given the wrong-sized shoes.

Dr. Bone was born in Budapest in 1889 and proved an intelligent—if disobedient—child. She wished to become a lawyer like her father, but this profession was closed to women. Her options were schoolmistress or doctor; she accepted the latter. Toting her great-grandfather's stethoscope and an ivory-handled Aesculapius stick, she enrolled in the medical faculty at Budapest University in the fall of 1908.

The Great War began soon after her graduation, and so she went to work in a military hospital. Perhaps it was there, seeing the suffering of the poorer classes, that her communist sympathies bloomed: she watched an illiterate Romanian soldier—a shepherd before the war—as he cried at the window for days, cradling a shattered arm and worrying about his lost children. He was only one broken man among many.

After the war, Dr. Bone devoted herself to Party work in England for sixteen years, and it was this foreign connection that would excite the suspicions of authorities when she returned to Communist Budapest in 1949.

Secret police stopped her at the airport on her way back to England; they packed her into their car and soon were driving her past a sheet-iron gate into their headquarters. "Haven't we conspired well?" joked the driver. "Nobody knows where you are." Indeed, her friends in England assumed she was staying on in Hungary and her friends in Hungary assumed she'd left for England. Dr. Bone just disappeared.

Inside headquarters, a slim man presented himself, decked in fine clothing and smooth manners. He took her into a little office and told her they knew she was a spy, an agent of the British secret service. "Until you tell us what your instructions were, you will not leave this building."

Dr. Bone replied: "In that case I shall probably die here, because I am not an agent of the secret service." She was then informed that her arrest was proof of guilt because the Party did not arrest innocent people.

She was escorted into the basement, and then into a narrow cell barely larger than its iron-framed bed. She could reach up and touch the ceiling. Much to the annoyance of her jailors, Dr. Bone lay herself down and fell immediately into a peaceful sleep. Later, she shivered from the cold and a guard mocked her: "Don't be afraid."

"I am not afraid," she told him.

What followed—her seven years and fifty-nine days of solitary confinement—is the stuff of horror films. She was held in filthy, freezing cells; the walls either dripped with water or were furred with fungus. She was generally half-starved and always isolated except when confronted by guards. Twenty-three ill-trained officers interrogated her with insults and threats—once for a sixty-hour stretch. For one period of six months, she was plunged into total darkness.

And yet her captors received no false confessions, no pleas for mercy; their only bounty was the tally of her insolent replies. It became a kind of recreation for Dr. Bone to annoy the prison authorities on the rare occasions when she saw them.

When she asked for a barber, her guards told her women must have long hair, so she spent three weeks tearing each hair individually until she had the short cut she preferred. In the summer of 1951 she went on a language strike, refusing to speak Hungarian ("their barbaric lingo," as she called it). She offered instead to speak German, French, Russian, English, or Italian—she was fluent in all five.

But Dr. Bone's most extraordinary stratagem was not the way she toyed with her captors—it was the way she held sway over her self. The dogged maintenance of her own sanity. From within that enforced void she slowly, steadily, built for herself an interior world that could not be destroyed or stripped from her. She recited poetry, for starters, translating the verses she knew by heart into each of her six languages. Then she began composing her own doggerel poems. One, made up during those six months without light, praised the saving grace of her mind's "dark-born magic wand."

Inspired by a prisoner she remembered from a Tolstoy story, Dr. Bone took herself on imaginary walks through all the cities she'd visited: she strolled the streets of Paris and Rome and Florence and Milan; she toured the Tiergarten in Berlin and Mozart's residence in Vienna. Later, while her feet wore a narrow furrow into the concrete beside her bed, she set out in her mind on a journey home to London. She walked a certain distance each day and kept a mental record of where she'd left off. She made the trip four times, each time stopping when she arrived at the Channel, as it seemed too cold to swim.

The accounting of these distances was too imprecise, though, so Dr. Bone decided she must have an abacus. She moulded bits of stale bread into beads and strung these along pieces of straw, which she stole from the broom that guards handed her when they told her to clean her cell. Now she could make calculations up to a trillion. On her abacus she proceeded to enumerate her vocabulary; she found that she knew 27,369 English words. She went on to tally her German, her French. And then, how many birds could she name (though she may never hear them)? How many trees (though she may never see them)? How many wines (though she may never taste them again)?

She moulded more bread crumbs into letters, four thousand in all, which she kept in twenty-six bread-crafted pigeonholes. This was her printing press of wheat, and she used it to spell out her ideas and her poetry. The guards, when they peered in, frowned and told her she was not normal. And Dr. Bone agreed.

She was given pills for her weakening digestion, and she found these included a green tint that she could use to dye her bread crumbs. And so she crafted miniature branches of holly at Christmastime. For their crimson berries, she bled.

Dr. Bone's guards were infuriated, but she proved to be proficient in the art of being alone. They cut her off from the world and she exercised that art, choosing peace over madness, consolation over despair, and solitude over imprisonment. Far from being destroyed, Dr. Bone emerged from prison (in her words) "a little wiser and full of hope."

By chance one day, I read a book that mentioned Dr. Bone in passing—just a line or two. I was amazed her story wasn't better known and I became determined to learn more. Eventually, I came across her memoir in a rare book collection at York University (*Seven Years Solitary* was published in 1957, just a year after her release). I found her story remarkable. Her writing was offhand and authentic enough that I imagined I knew her voice—comically stern, and marbled by a youth spent in the Hungary that turned so viciously against her. As I became more familiar with her attitude toward solitary confinement—and her bottomless capacity to endure it—I felt a creeping kind of envy coming over me. I wasn't envious of her circumstances, of course. But I was envious of her faculties. Was there, I wondered, any part of my world that inspired the accumulation of mental reserves like hers? Or would I always be fleeing the prison of myself—a luxury Dr. Bone was not afforded?

Even the handful of solitary hours it took to read her story were difficult for me to endure. I kept looking up, hoping for interruption from the hushed student librarians in the next room, wondering if a sociable scholar might plop down at the long table where I worked. I fidgeted and felt ashamed as I compared myself to the formidable Dr. Bone.

At last her story was done and I slapped shut the papers and books, wandered out into prickling white afternoon sun. But that uneasiness didn't dissipate the way I thought it would. As I wove myself into streams of students, as I jostled my way to the crowded café and out onto a packed bus, the problem wouldn't stop pinging in the back of my head. I wanted more time to myself but always balked when I got it. This was a problem worth tackling. More than that. Dr. Bone's brilliant mode of being—her confidence in the richness of her own, interior life—was something worth importing to our obsessively connected world.

How to be alone. And why.

There must be an art to it, I thought. A certain practice, or alchemy, that turns loneliness into solitude, blank days into blank canvases. It must be one of those lost arts, like svelte calligraphy or the confident tying of a wedding cravat. A lost little art that, year by year, fades in the bleaching light of the future.

Part I

The Uses of Solitude

I believe I know the only cure, which is to make one's center of life inside of one's self, not selfishly or excludingly, but with a kind of unassailable serenity—to decorate one's inner house so richly that one is content there, glad to welcome anyone who wants to come and stay, but happy all the same when one is inevitably alone.

—*Edith Wharton*

I

All Together Now

My partner, Kenny, maintains a kind of detached interest in whatever I'm writing. ("Detached" because he knows better than to encourage a writer at the dinner table.) But when I told him Dr. Bone's story and said I'd like to write something about solitude, he put down his beer and looked at me. "Have you even been alone before? For longer than—I don't know—a day? Really alone?"

Now my own glass was down and I frowned into middle distance. "I must have been. . . ." But of course I hadn't, not really. He suggested, with annoying saneness, that I might want to try it.

I pivoted the conversation, but it was impossible to ignore that a gauntlet had been tossed. My eyes narrowed. Kenny would be away the following week, and I silently pledged to spend a day entirely alone—with neither people nor their digital avatars making any contact.

When the day arrived, however, a text came at 9 a.m., and I checked it as though fulfilling some Pavlovian law. An offer to drink in the park with friends from out of town. Disaster!

I cheated. And then I cheated again. I went to the café. I answered a call from my mom. I went on a jog and stopped to pet a puppy. By bedtime I counted up a dozen interactions in all. I couldn't even be alone for one day.

I might have the wherewithal to leave the phone at home sometimes, to slightly curb my media gluttony, but real removal from the demands of society? This was a sensation—barely remembered—from childhood, from a time I could go hiking into the woods with my Polaroid camera and forget, for hours, about the existence of other humans.

I had changed—just grown older—and I'd acquired the webs and wires that tie adults to each other. I woke one day to find that those empty spaces had been filled in with nervous worries about the development of my friends' children, about the happiness of far-flung relatives, about the security of my peers in a precarious economy—and to this was added more selfish worries about my reputation (my sketchy "brand"), which could be bruised at any point by a crude remark online or a gossipy insinuation. In short, I had become enmeshed.

Then again, maybe it was the world that had changed; perhaps it no longer made allowances for solitude in the same way. Or perhaps, more likely, it was a combination of the two forces—my own growing older and the world's self-tethering to online things. It had all changed, within and without, so that now, in a haze of social anxiety, I woke each morning thinking, "What did I miss?" and went to bed thinking, "What did I say?"

The crowd, that smorgasbord of perpetual connection, left me hungry. In fact, I realized, I'd been hungry for years. But now that hunger was putting me to work. A little reading—and a hero in Dr. Bone—had turned a malaise into a mission. I wanted to become acquainted again with the still night, with my own hapless daydreaming, with the bare self I had (for how long?) been running from. I kept asking myself: why am I so afraid of my own quiet company? This book is the closest I've come to an answer.

To be clear: none of what follows is a pining for Thoreau's old cabin in the woods. I don't want to run away from the world—I want to rediscover myself within it. I want to know what happens if we again take doses of solitude from inside our crowded days, along our crowded streets.

It's not so easy. I step outside, intent on a solitary ramble, and I compulsively observe the social exchanges of others. A forlorn teenaged couple coos on the sidewalk, performing their morning farewell; on the nearby grass, a mother plays peekaboo with her eternally delighted infant; a rabbi gets in his Audi while managing someone on the phone; a woman leans out the window of a coffee van and passes a macchiato to her customer, chirping, "Beautiful coffee for a beautiful lady." Everywhere and anywhere, we groom each other. Indeed, it's with these soft but persistent offerings that we ensure the survival of our culture and our species.

———

Living in large groups, we have learned, puts a major tax on any animal's brain—in particular on its neocortex. In fact, all the markers of social complexity among primates—their group size, grooming cliques, mating strategies, tactical deception, and social play—are strongly correlated with the relative size of that primate's neocortex. The bigger the neocortex, the more social the primate. The more social the primate, the larger the group they can live in without having that group implode with violence and fractious behaviour.

The data bears this out. Anthropologist Robin Dunbar, in developing his "social brain" theory in the 1990s, found that the relative size of a simian's neocortex was directly related to how large their groups became: night monkeys and tamarins, for example, have small neocortices relative to their brain size and hang out in numbers less than ten; chimpanzees and baboons have relatively large neocortices and have groups of fifty-plus. Humans, for the vast majority of our history, have hung out in groups of around 150—and we also (no surprise) have the largest proportionate neocortex of any primate. Dunbar argues that our big brains may well have helped us become tool users, but the real advantage was that we became able to increase the size of the communities we live in. More peers means more safety, more strength, more chances to pass on wisdom, and, ultimately, more chances for survival.

Something else Dunbar discovered was that the larger a primate group becomes, the more time it devotes to social grooming. All those affections, frustrations, and aggressions need to be perpetually monitored and managed. Surviving in a large group of primates is a sophisticated bit of work. Depending on group size, the amount of time primates spend grooming each other can reach 20 per cent of a given day.[1] Dunbar was struck by the fact that, given our enormous social groups, today's human animal should be forced to "groom" for enormous portions of each day. So how did we get around Dunbar's rule? How did we manage to grow our social groups without being forced to spend all our time picking proverbial lice out of each other's hair?

The answer lies in the game-changing emergence of language, perhaps a hundred thousand years ago. The preverbal primate must lay hands on a friend or foe in order to groom them. A primate that can speak, that can make complex social suggestions beyond raw vocalization, can in effect "groom" several members of his or her social group at once. This is a powerful bit of multiplication. What's more, a talking ape is not stuck squatting in the weeds while grooming; the talking ape can groom while out on a walk or while foraging for berries. *This* is a powerful bit of multitasking. The birth of language made grooming highly efficient and viral.[2] With language, our ancestors could export complex thoughts from one mind to another, enabling the coordination of hunting and foraging, and eventually farming. With language we could maintain the stability (and thus the rewards) of larger and larger social groups.

And we didn't stop there. We continued to discover new ways to expand and highlight our social grooming; and so the human animal (toting that mammoth-sized neocortex) was able to live in larger and larger groups while keeping some semblance of structure and safety intact. By this reckoning, every piece of communication technology—from papyrus to the printing press to Pinterest—has hijacked an elemental part of our minds. These technologies, in turn, magnify our ability to groom each other, enabling us to develop enormous cities, and eventually "the global village." We experience empathy or hatred for humans on the other side of the planet—refugees and terrorists that we'll never even meet. As I write this sentence there are an estimated 7,401,858,841 living humans, and, for the first time in history, each is potentially connected to all the others; that makes 27,393,757,147,344,002,220 possible connections.* So, as I sit here, alone in my little office—my cell—the world outside buzzes with more than 27 quintillion possible greetings.

This change is, of course, not yet spread uniformly across the planet. As William Gibson said, "The future is already here, it's just not evenly distributed." Indeed, many iPhone junkies are surprised when informed that less than half of the world's population has access to the Internet. That said, the change comes fast, and neither poverty nor rural isolation will keep populations offline for long: in 2006, 18 per cent of the world was online; by 2009, 25 per cent were; and by 2014, the number had climbed to 41 per cent.[3] Such a growth rate is phenomenal. Consider how messaging systems, which dominate this new reality and represent our most direct act of online social grooming, so quickly propagate: WhatsApp, a

---

* Between n nodes there are $(n\text{-}1)n/2$ connections.

kingpin of instant message platforms, reached one billion users in 2016.

Aristotle defined humans as social animals and he was only too right. Making sure other people have positive impressions of us is one of our central motivations. And when we use screen-based social media instead of face-to-face interactions to groom each other, we're able to be more strategic about that self-presentation. For example, when confronted with a Facebook post about someone's new job, my lovely but nervous friend Jocelyn may write and rewrite her comment for several minutes before finally landing on the tapioca-scale inoffensiveness of "So happy for you!!!" (If she's feeling crazy, Jocelyn may add a martini glass emoji.) Unsurprisingly, a 2015 study found that, of the roughly 1.5 billion regular Facebook users, usage spikes among those with social anxiety—in particular, those who have a high need for social assurance.[4] The technology becomes a salve, a way to calm our worries about fitting in or belonging. And, with astonishing speed, the compulsion to groom online has been absorbed into our idea of the natural: Only 8 per cent of adults in the United States used social networking sites in 2005; that number blew up to 73 per cent by 2013.[5] Meanwhile, nearly half of Americans now sleep with their phones on their bedside tables, using them as surrogate teddy bears. To be human is to be social; to be human in the age of screens is to be massively social.

And yet. . . . In the same way that many people are forced to engineer healthy diets for themselves in a world overflowing with the salts and sugars and fats we're designed to hoard, it's possible that we're such compulsive social groomers that we now must keep ourselves from gobbling the fast-food equivalent. Has social media made us socially obese—gorged on constant connection but never properly nourished?

Has the neocortex—the very thing that made us human, the thing that kickstarted our cities and our politics, our religions and our art—been hijacked one too many times?

When did the online grooming impulse really get scary, though? It's a parlour game to mark these things, but here's a shot: 9:49 a.m. on July 14, 2004. That was the moment a fellow logged onto a site devoted to advice about digital video files and launched a new chat forum with the words, "i am lonely will anyone speak to me." A decade later, *Salon* crowned the string of commentary that resulted "the saddest thread on the Internet." But even a few days after the initial posting, anyone who typed "I am lonely" into Google's search engine was taken there; folks left posts about their own crushing loneliness and earned some small commiseration. It turns out that many people, a couple of glasses of solo Shiraz into the night, will find themselves casting the words "I am lonely" into the Internet's waters. But what do they expect to reel back? *We are all losers and need lives,* typed one visitor. *It's as if no one is real anymore,* wrote another. Nobody asked about psychiatrists and medication, nor were they searching for a boyfriend or non-smoker housemate. This was, instead, just a digital howl.

It's not so odd to ask the Internet to solve the problem of human loneliness. I've grown accustomed to phrasing Google searches as helpless questions. I might type, "What time is it in Paris?" Or, "How many ounces are in a litre?" These are called oracular searches (as in "ask the oracle"). It's a simple slip to then submit a more emotional query to such an authority. *Why aren't I happy? Why does nobody love me?*

9:49 a.m., July 14, 2004. A dull Wednesday morning. Perhaps that was the moment the online grooming impulse got out of hand. An anonymous guy—let's call him Eddie—felt lonely and it occurred to him he might turn to the Internet for company. It was easy. And the oracle was inviting. "I am lonely will anyone speak to me." There was nothing terribly new about Eddie's desire to bolt from his own company; what was new was the ease, the technology's soft promise that he never needed to feel lonely again. If the Internet had become a demolisher of solitude, then it wasn't an uninvited one. We had already learned to be grateful for its little intrusions, its smiling impositions.

By 2020, anywhere from thirty billion to fifty billion objects—cars, toasters, shampoo bottles—will be connected to the Internet; that is triple the number of online things available as of this writing, in 2016.[6] Once insensate items in your bedroom, your local park, the airplane toilet, will be sparked with an animating force that would have caused previous generations to marvel. (Certain members of the MIT Media Lab have taken to calling these things "enchanted objects"—which calls up Arthur C. Clarke's remark that "any sufficiently advanced technology is indistinguishable from magic.") This burgeoning Internet of Everything, wherein disconnection becomes a kind of sin, will rely on ties of constant connection and feedback—a permanent social vibe. Our environments, in other words, will be built less out of bricks and plastic and more out of cloud-based infrastructure.* These digital environments will balk at disconnection, seeing it as a breed of malfunction; the result will be a mental ecosystem that does likewise.

The beginnings of the Internet of Everything are already here. We build it by imbuing our parking meters, power grids, currency, automobiles, documents, pantries, clothing, and jewellery with an online intelligence that was unthinkable twenty years ago. Meanwhile, Google Now prompts me with an endless supply of cheerful, location-specific advice. Amazon's voice-activated Echo manages household tasks like a cloud-based servant, reordering supplies, maintaining shopping lists, and reading out recipes. Amazon Prime Air is desperate to deliver packages via drones. And self-learning

---

* This distinction is, of course, a kind of lie. We *perceive* a difference between the hard analogue world and the ethereal cloud-based world, but online things still live somewhere—in hard and real and energy-sucking servers.

home appliances track the activities of humans, syncing their behaviour in an attempt to make their functionality as invisible as possible. We're often not aware of our position in this spiral of connections, but we have daily proof (if we look for it) that the bias of our hours has swung away from solitude and toward enmeshment.

Nor is such cyborg glory the domain of human habitats alone. We shall make over the animal kingdom in our image. Some Swiss dairy cows, for instance, send text messages to their farmers via sensors and SIM cards that are implanted in the animals' necks. These devices can tell when the cows are in heat. The message, more or less, reads: "I am ready to be inseminated."[7] Eat your heart out, Tinder.

I cannot speak for the cows, but humans easily accept the bias toward connecting everything and everyone. As Dunbar's research made clear, this urge is built into our most basic nature. Of course, we're not alone in this; many species are social. But humans are one of a select few that qualify as *eu*social (*eu* meaning "true"). It's a term the great entomologist E. O. Wilson uses to describe a self-sacrificing, multigenerational network of animals. Like the ants that Wilson studies, we humans are super-cooperators. We're designed to constantly give way to the needs of the larger community. We're certainly capable of selfishness, too, but it's astounding how often we set aside our I-minded drive to sacrifice ourselves in service to the military conquests of others; how often we serve at the altar of collective projects as humble as an elementary school choir or as awe-inspiring as the creation of the Large Hadron Collider. To Wilson, the evolution of eusocial culture is "one of the major innovations in the history of life" (up there with the emergence of wings and flowers).[8]

Those intense social ties then conceal other modes of being: we humans now crowd out solitude at every opportunity. A 2013 survey of nearly 7,500 American smartphone users found that 80 per cent were on their phones within fifteen minutes of waking up.[9] The number rises to 89 per cent among eighteen- to twenty-four-year-olds (most of whom reach for the phone immediately upon waking). In fact, one out of four respondents could not recall a time in the day when their phone was not in arm's reach. This is a eusocial commitment if ever there was one. Our extension into massive social networks stretches far beyond practicality; it's utterly compulsive and compulsory, a phantom umbilical cord. Type "fear of being" into Google and it auto-completes to "fear of being alone."

Meanwhile, type "fear of being without" and it auto-completes to "fear of being without a cellphone." Many decry the rise of FOMO—fear of missing out—but, for me, this phrase doesn't capture the breadth of the anxiety. When I go out walking without my phone for an hour or two, it's a fear of missing *myself*, and not the news, that charges my nerves. Like a lover who can see himself only under the lamp of the beloved's attention, I seem to be always in danger of disappearing when away from the notice of others.

It doesn't help matters that hits of social grooming via our phones release dopamine in our brains, activating our pleasure/reward system.* When I spoke with psychologist Elizabeth Waterman, who specializes in these addictions, she told me, "We are simply hard-wired to share for our own survival." And the more we share, the better we feel—in the short term at least: "The reward system in the brain lights up when we know that information of ours has been shared with many people as opposed to it just being shared with a few." The primate's chest pumps up as it grooms an entire crowd. Who on Twitter hasn't felt that jolt of dopamine when an expertly "offhand" remark gets multiple retweets?

Tellingly, our digital desires are focused almost exclusively on the social. Waterman told me that it's mostly social media apps that leave people at risk for addiction: "It's texting,

---

* The very DNA of the Internet appears to be one long extension of our social instincts—strung with electric ones and zeros. The Internet's godfather, the ARPANET, was built by academics who believed the sharing of information would be an enormous boon, precipitating a second enlightenment. The project was funded by a U.S. Congress that believed in its military necessity (you can't blow up a dispersed communication system with a single bomb), but the academics at work touted a less brutal philosophy—they championed the open exchange of information and the decentralization of authority. It was an ethic they inherited, in fact, from the original Enlightenment. And always, always there was the expectation that conversation (not content) would be king. "On the Internet," writes *Boing Boing* editor Cory Doctorow, "every medium is first a medium for social conversation and secondarily a specialized forum for some other purpose." In other words, whatever we are doing, we're sharing it.

Instagram, Pinterest, and the rest. By contrast, there's basically no risk of addiction from non-social sites that deal with
the news, or weather, or sports results. It is the sharing itself
that is addictive." Waterman's point gives a finer definition to
the vague anxiety I get when looking at my phone—an anxiety I see mirrored in others. It's this adolescent urge to be
needed, connected, loved—and, yes, groomed—all poured
into a shining totem. All poured into this black enigma. So
small in the hand yet hinting at overwhelming realities. In
particular, economic ones.

Those of us born in the twentieth century grew up in an economy dominated by energy and banking. But a new player has
arisen this past decade—the platform. And platform companies are, above all else, social. Whereas "pipeline" companies
of old would build something and sell you that something
(*Want some Nikes? Here's some Nikes*), a platform company—like Uber or YouTube—simply builds the factory and
invites you, the user, to do the labour. *You* drive the car, *you*
make the video—and the platform company will take its cut.
Many platforms do not pay anything for this labour, but the
joy of sharing, we are assured, will be its own reward. This
is an extremely useful arrangement for the platform owner—
it doesn't require much overhead. When Instagram, for
example, was sold to Facebook for $1 billion in the spring of
2012, it had only thirteen employees. All of the actual value
in the company was created, free of charge, by its masses of

users—a grateful and industrious public. As of this writing, over a billion users are uploading more than four hundred hours of video to YouTube *every minute*. Paying for that kind of labour would make a platform like YouTube untenable. But getting users to perform the labour for free turns a platform into a platinum mine.

It is platforms that have produced the cutely titled "sharing economy," too: we can rent a stranger's apartment via Airbnb; we can borrow tools from folks across town on SnapGoods; we can share bikes or cars thanks to RelayRides or Wheelz. It can seem, at first blush, fairly utopian. How convivial! All we needed was a way to share! (Never mind that the sharing economy often exists outside of formal taxation structures, so that society at large does not partake in the "sharing.") Cracks soon appear. For example, the sharing economy also provides for an app like MonkeyParking, which, in 2014, allowed people to auction off parking spots in San Francisco to the highest bidder—before the city attorney stepped in and insisted that the City by the Bay would not abide a system where the wealthy park where they like and poor citizens are shoved aside.[10]

Simultaneously, a new class of "precariat" (a portmanteau of *precarious* and *proletariat*) has emerged, characterized by sketchy and ever-changing job lives. It is expected that half the American workforce will be freelancers by 2020.[11] A growing proportion of those will be crowd-workers that serve as cogs in the platform economy, perhaps performing a string of endless gigs doled out by the likes of Uber or TaskRabbit, and perhaps employed by less well-branded companies that have them doing data entry or scouring LinkedIn as human search engines. These workers are tethered only in an ethereal way to their employers; they are anonymous and they are stripped of health care, retirement packages, and other benefits that previous generations took for granted. The freedom associated with freelancing—the happy-go-lucky life advertised by "hives" of shared workspace—is a hollow freedom if you have to sing for every element of your supper.

I spoke about these changes with Marshall Van Alstyne, a bright-eyed professor at Boston University and MIT who focuses on the economics of digital business. "About thirteen of the top thirty companies are now platform companies," he told me. "It's a much more dramatic shift than most people give it credit for." In fact, Van Alstyne feels the shift we're undergoing is analogous to the transition at the turn of the previous century—the Industrial Revolution. "At that point," he explained, "you saw massive capital infrastructure being built for iron, for oil, for copper. But it's no longer about supply economies of scale—it's *demand* economies of scale. The users themselves now create the value." Van Alstyne believes that, over the next decade, platforms will become the dominant firms in the economy.

He further believes that the platform approach to organization will extend beyond mere businesses to shape whole cities and governments. (His colleagues at MIT are already working with the governments of Singapore, London, Copenhagen, and Seattle.) These would be whole "intelligent" communities. If platform companies rely on users to run things, the same can be said for a "platform city"—vast urban arrangements will rely on data input from crowds of citizens to optimize the delivery of transportation, policing, retail, tourism, and more. Citizen behaviour is turned into data, which is dispersed by apps and dashboards to (presumably) retailers, governments, and the citizens themselves. Imagine, for example, "smart sewage": MIT's Senseable City Lab is developing an open-data platform that monitors human waste in real time, allowing dynamic new approaches to epidemiology in cities. (Immediate data on disease outbreaks is one obvious benefit.) The movements of crowds, taxis, airline passengers, and shipping containers could all become available, too, so the city could react to its own patterns.[12]

As optimistic as a platform-based city might sound, I wonder if this shift will undo an essential quality of city living. For didn't some of us move to the city in the first place to become anonymous, to be uncounted, to go solo amidst a disorganized crowd—and thus, to find *ourselves*, lest we be informed too much by the findings of others?

The vision of a platform city—synchronized, social, and seamless—feels at once utopian and Orwellian. It's a vision of a future where politics, economics, and culture all bend beneath that primal desire to connect at every opportunity.

Meanwhile, if I covet a little alone time, if I detach without permission from that great heaving crowd, I am presumed to be a lost person. Even as I began work on this book I was hassled for seizing small opportunities, little dodges from connection. I'd take a day to respond to a text or turn down an invitation, saying, "No real reason—just feel like staying in tonight." And people *hated* it. One friend asked what he'd done to make me lose interest in pub nights. Another became furious when I didn't respond to a wedding announcement on his Facebook page. (I hadn't been on Facebook for seven years, but that didn't matter: he expected to be monitored.) My task was to get over *their* discomfort as much as my own. There's a real taboo involved in solitude.

But taboos are made to be broken. We're given opportunities to practise being alone every day, almost every hour. Go on a drive. Sit on a lawn. Stick your phone in a drawer. Once we start looking, we find solitude is always just below the surface of things. I thought at first that solitude was a lost art. Now I know that's too pretty a term, too soft a metaphor.

Solitude has become a resource.

Like all resources, it can be harvested and hoarded, taken up by powerful forces without permission or inquiry, and then transformed into private wealth, until the fields of empty space we once took for granted first dwindle, then disappear. Ultimately, we lose the capacity to develop a rich interior life like Dr. Bone's.

There are benefits to maintaining this resource—as sure as there are benefits to maintaining our oceans and forests. But we won't bother to protect our solitude until we recall that it has a value.

———

True solitude—as opposed to the failed solitude that we call loneliness—is a fertile state, yet one we have a hard time accessing. Once we do make room for it, though, we discover there are needful things hidden in that empty space, still waiting between the flash and action of our social lives. As my research continued, I began to remember a calm separateness, a sureness I once could live inside for an easy hour at a time. I couldn't wait to meet myself again.

2

What Is Solitude For?

I was shocked when my older brother, on a visit to our apartment, let his infant son crawl around the corner and out of sight. I became incapable of focusing on our conversation, sure that Levi was nibbling a frayed wire or blithely rolling in broken glass. I couldn't stand that he might live a single minute unmonitored. And, in my anxiety, I was in good company. We're told that even God, the original parent, fretted after placing Adam alone in the Garden of Eden: "It is not good that the man should be alone," he intoned. It's a worry that consumes the neophyte.

Studies of animals, though, show that parents will deliberately leave their offspring alone in order to let them grow. Meanwhile, the nervous human parent often fails to provide any alone time at all. A baby turns and stares into space and its mother thrusts a spinning toy or mirror before its eyes, thwarting the infant's ability to self-regulate levels of stimulus or sociability.*

Many feel that only contact with other people can produce thoughts and feelings in the infant. But the star psychologist Ester Buchholz's work pointed out that newborns actually arrive more inner-directed than outer. Indeed, with the advent of intrauterine photography we learned that a fourteen-week-old fetus will satisfy its own urges by sucking its thumb, long before it ever has access to a breast.

We are not simply ready-made social animals—our caretakers often work quite hard to "civilize" us, making us more social than is our wont. "We are born," insists Buchholz, "ready to do things on our own as well as to connect to others. Both needs—to be alone and to engage—are essential." Without solitude, the child fails to become self-governing, and "there is no denying that many of our social and psychological 'diseases' are primarily disturbances in self-regulation."[13]

Even when we've grown, lamented Buchholz, society simply refuses to *let* people be mateless. "All the push, all the time, is toward relationships, and if you resist that you're just considered antisocial or crazy." She was amazed to find that few people recognize both connection and disconnection as elements in our happiness and survival.[14]

---

* Paradoxically, such perpetual social grooming can lead to deep loneliness later in life, when that level of attention is found wanting and the grown child suffers what psychoanalyst Gregory Zilboorg called "egotistic desolation."

Now, as we pack our lives with digital company along with the flesh-and-blood sort, we reach a threshold after which more "contact" creates only an odd kind of loneliness, a crowd-sickness. We groom and get groomed but receive diminishing returns and, despite constantly feeding on social fuel, we remain unsatisfied. Thoreau complained that "we meet at meals three times a day and give each other a new taste of that old musty cheese that we are."[15] But three times a day sounds like a Buddhist retreat to me. My contact with friends and family has ballooned to something far more pernicious: an ambient, nervous, and constant awareness of each other. We take up this impoverished plenitude because it's easier and more comforting than the rich scarcity we left behind.

We take it up because we think that companionship is an alternative to solitude—that the big black hole at the centre of our selves can eventually be topped up if we just shovel enough sugary society into it. But the alternative to solitude was never companionship. The alternative to solitude is loneliness.

Loneliness is on the rise. Among middle-aged and older Americans, rates of loneliness have jumped from 14 per cent in the 1970s to over 40 per cent today.[16] Even by 2004, the National Science Foundation reported in its General Social Survey that the number of Americans who called themselves lonely was skyrocketing. More than a quarter of their 1,500 interviewees stated that they had nobody to discuss their trials and triumphs with (this number is three times higher than in the 1984 survey).[17] Meanwhile, in *The Insecure American*, editors Hugh Gusterson and Catherine Besteman paint a portrait of a people terrified of "the other," retreating into gated communities and writhing in paranoia about terrorists and job-stealing foreigners. This is the world Robert Putnam describes in *Bowling Alone*: "Over the course of the last generation or two, a variety of technological, economic, and social changes have rendered obsolete the stuff of American social capital."[18] By 2013, the *New York Times* could argue that more Americans die from weak social ties (leading to suicide) than from car crashes.[19] All this despite a massive uptick in tech-aided "connection." Tellingly, when a team at Oregon Health and Science University tracked eleven thousand adults between 2004 and 2010, they found that phone calls made little difference to their risk for depression. And as for emails and texts? They had no effect on depression levels whatsoever.[20] It seems that becoming the most connected humans in history is no guarantee against isolation.

The common cure for loneliness is more connections, yet exercising our solitude is another option. Time alone is inevitable—but can we thrive when it occurs? If we have failed to do so, perhaps it's because we don't see the point—we've forgotten solitude's value. So: what *is* solitude for?

Its first great use was detailed in the work of the renowned psychiatrist Anthony Storr, who was responding to a 1980s culture where "the telephone is an ever-present threat to privacy" and "the menace of 'Muzak' has invaded shops, hotels, aircraft, and even elevators."[21] There, in the comparatively peaceful eighties, Storr watched the empty corners in his life fill up with stuff. The menacing Muzak was as much an assault on his solitary mind as an Android jiggling with push alerts is on yours and mine. Each generation has its own expectation of solitude—and each expectation is assaulted in its turn. In the 1930s, even so urbane a voice as the *New York Times* was disgusted by the "terrible intimacy" that the rise of radio and television allowed amongst a "mixed" audience.[22]

What did Storr really worry about, after we peel back the moralizing of his time? What great thing was that constant stream of media and voice flushing from modern lives? He believed that the greatest benefit of solitude is its ability to engender new ideas. A leading scholar of his day, Storr analyzed the lives of great artists—Beethoven, Dostoyevsky, Kafka, Sexton, the list goes on—with a psychiatrist's eye. And he found that the eureka moment ("aha moment" in today's Oprah terms) does not occur at conference tables. Why does the Buddha meditate alone beneath a tree? Why does Jesus spend forty days in the wilderness? Why does Muhammad withdraw for the month of Ramadan? For that matter, why do so many tribal cultures incorporate a solitary quest into a child's rite of passage? Solitude is built into the stories we tell ourselves about illumination.

A retreat from the crowds has always been necessary for the formulation of brave new ideas, Storr explains, with "nearly all kinds of creative people, in adult life, [showing] some avoidance of others, some need of solitude."[23] The cliché of the painter locked away in a studio, the writer in his cabin, the scientist in her late-night laboratory, is no accident. And Storr's assertion was backed up in 1994 when the psychologist Mihaly Csikszentmihalyi (the originator of the concept of "flow" in work) found that teenagers who can't stand being alone tend to have lessened creative abilities.[24] Only in solitude could those youths develop the creative habits—journalling, doodling, daydreaming—that lead to original work.

Our best thinkers may also crave solitude because, as Storr notes, "ideas are sensitive plants which wilt if exposed to premature scrutiny."[25] And so children shield their hand-made birthday cards or bits of craftwork from prying family members, exclaiming: "It's not ready!" And so adults frown at dinner parties to see their spontaneous thoughts mauled by the wolves of other people's misunderstanding.

But fresh ideas are only one benefit of solitude. Knowledge of the self—or even self-therapy—is another gain. The word *retreat* was traditionally used to mean a beneficial withdrawal, perhaps to a spa or place of vacation. But contemporary health practitioners largely ignore the benefits of solitude for the distressed: we rush toward group therapy, talk therapy, and any means at all to keep the mentally ill socially occupied. Although this approach may be beneficial for schizophrenics, not everyone needs more socialization. Indeed, many of us are desperately in need of isolation. Removing oneself from every-day society, says Storr, "promotes self-understanding and con-tact with those inner depths of being which elude one in the hurly-burly of day-to-day life."[26] Key research has emerged since Storr wrote, showing that solitude enhances one's mental freedom, unshackling us by minimizing the intrusive self-consciousness that the presence of others inevitably produces.[27] We might know this intuitively, but researchers—notably Reed W. Larson—have confirmed our assumptions: when study populations were randomly contacted over the course of many days and asked to report on their status, researchers found that, yes, we seek out solitude when we need free rein in both our thoughts and actions.

And yet being confronted by our bare selves can so often feel bracing, even frightening. Larson points out, "To take advantage of the opportunities afforded by solitude, a person must be able to turn a basically terrifying state of being into a productive one."[28] The nervy stress of it all can reach existential proportions. Comedian Louis C.K., riffing on the need to check cellphones during solo car rides, described perfectly our need to dodge the solitary self. He achieved a certain poeticism when he said on *Late Night with Conan O'Brien*:

> Underneath everything in your life there is that thing, that empty—forever empty. That knowledge that it's all for nothing and you're alone. It's down there. And sometimes when things clear away and you're not watching and you're in your car and you start going, 'Ooh, here it comes, that I'm alone,' like it starts to visit on you, just this sadness. Life is tremendously

sad, just by being in it. . . . That's why we text and drive. . . . People are willing to risk taking a life and ruining their own because they don't want to be alone for a second because it's so hard.[29]

Studies show we're impaired for fifteen full seconds after we text while driving[30]—but this "deadly wandering" (as Matt Richtel termed it) is a small price to a person fleeing their own loneliness.

The naked self, then, is a bogeyman. Yet facing up to it can eventually become a numinous encounter. This is the achievement that Jung described as "individuation"—the ability to appreciate yourself as a creature separate from your species. As Jung has it: "a being distinct from the general, collective psychology"[31] will experience "an enriching of conscious psychological life;"[32] being a true individual is a "coming to selfhood or 'self-realization.'"[33] In other words, solitude relieves us from a nervous hive mentality; it reminds us the self is no monster after all.

These benefits—fresh ideas and self-knowledge—are then joined by one final benefit: bonding with others. At first this seems a paradox: how can solitude better our relations with people when the paradigmatic experience of solitude is disengagement? But there's an important distinction to be made: social disengagement does not preclude other types of engagement. Removing ourselves from the presence of others does not mean we aren't engaged in what's called "indirect or sub-stitutive engagement."[34] Step away from a party and you may think more clearly about the charming fellow you met there. Say goodbye to your mother and you may spend the next five minutes feeling grateful for her attention.[*]

Besides, the person who knows how to be properly alone is never completely alone. We each carry with us the comfort and knowledge of those we've loved and who have cared for us. Without this remembrance, our solitude would be unbearable. The English psychoanalyst Donald Winnicott made the point in 1958 that loneliness and anxiety are avoided in healthy individuals by unconsciously accessing the parental, caregiving experience of childhood. "The basis of the capacity to be alone," writes Winnicott, "is a para-dox." The mother (or a mother-substitute) is understood to be available, though not immediately engaging. "Without a sufficiency of this experience," he explains, "the capacity to be alone cannot develop."[35] He noticed in healthy babies a state he called "going-on-being," in which the child is calm and the parent does not demand their attention—in this state a sense of self begins to coalesce.[36] It can happen later in life, too. Patients in analysis sometimes learn to be alone in the presence of a caretaker when they have a "silent session," in

---

[*] I originally wondered whether a text message could count as "indirect engagement," but I think it cannot. Text messages, despite the absence of the interlocutor, are direct engagements. A memory of a loved one, by contrast, remains indirect because it is contained, felt by the solitary person alone; the experience must be independent.

which they lie on the sofa and say nothing to their analyst. (Indeed, entire symposia have been mounted to study the significance of the silences that patients and analysts produce.) The ability to be alone, then, is anything but a rejection of close bonds. It's an affirmation of those bonds on the most essential level.* To be happily alone is to affirm one's faith in the love of others. My brother was quite right to let little Levi be.

Each time we write a letter, or reminisce about friends on a solitary walk, we reaffirm those bonds. We prove our faith in others—prove it and thus strengthen it—when we calmly experience separation.

I was walking through Vancouver's leafy West End with an ex-boyfriend recently; he'd just returned from a year working in China. (The Great Firewall of China had made access to Facebook, Twitter, and Instagram all but impossible.) He turned to me on the sidewalk and said: "It's weird, but I had to go to a city as populated as Shanghai to feel the quiet in my brain that I'd been craving. And now, being back, it's so great. I can always tell when I'm real friends with somebody because it doesn't bother me when we're apart. I know we'll meet again and pick up exactly where we were." And we did. It was precisely Winnicott's point: only someone who

---

* Eric Klinenberg, in *Going Solo*, argues that our ability to be happily alone is actually a sign of *strong* social ties, not a lack thereof. He notes, for example, that the countries with the highest rates of solo living—Sweden, Norway, Finland, and Denmark—are all countries famed for their communal support.

feels at risk of being abandoned would be uneasy with periodic detachment.

These, then, are solitude's uses: new ideas; an understanding of the self; and closeness to others. Taken together, these three ingredients build a rich interior life. It turns out that merely escaping crowds was never the point of solitude at all: rather, solitude is a resource—an ecological niche—inside of which these benefits can be reaped. And so it matters enormously when that resource is under attack.

"I love to be alone," says Thoreau. "I never found the companion that was so companionable as solitude."[37] That is from *Walden*, which was published in 1854. How swiftly, how irrevocably the world swung toward permanent social contact after that moment. *Walden* is a swan song for an antique enjoyment of time alone (so naive by today's standards that at one point Thoreau complains that distant train whistles are an intolerable invasion of his peace). The "picture telegraph," which anticipated television, was invented the very next year; the transatlantic telegraph cable was laid the next decade; the telephone was invented a decade after that. In short order, Thoreau's idea of solitude flashed one final time and receded into the night—for it had become, to some extent, moot. The crowd marched inexorably forward, sweeping more and more of us into its magnetic mass. And, to make room for that mass, our solitude was chopped down.

———

The truth is, as I began writing this book I was dreading the time I'd be spending alone. The interminable months of reading and scribbling, the tired eyes staring out windows, the blank hours prone on the sofa. Writing a book is about the most solitary activity a person can opt for. Every morning you pour the coffee, squint at the blazing white screen, and struggle against the sinking sense that you've dropped from the world's notice. . . . I twist in my chair, wonder who I can call or email. But then comes the needful denial. To write is to divorce the world and temporarily marry an idea of it instead.

It took weeks, months, for my attitude to even start to shift. As I spoke with experts about the insidious ways that new technologies teach us to fear our solitude, I realized I was bored by all this running from myself; I also realized I was getting angry. Angry because part of my life had been stolen from me. So I set myself looking for those lost pieces of solitude in every corner of my world. The pieces were waiting on subway rides, in sleepy mornings, on simple walks to the grocery store. Moments of solitude started showing up everywhere, as though a bag of jewels had been ripped open and it had all tumbled into tall grasses. And I wasn't the only one rediscovering things: some friends were so sick of their hyper-social lives that they were starting to opt out, too— nobody who did cried *lonely*. Bit by bit, we were stealing back our solitude.

Here's the rub: while forests and oceans may be preserved by the efforts of agencies and governments, the experience of solitude is by definition a personal one, so the struggle to preserve it must largely come from an individual. It's no longer enough to simply note the benefits of disconnection. Our online crowds are so insistent, so omnipresent, that we now must actively elbow out the forces that encroach on solitude's borders, or else forfeit to them a large portion of our mental landscape. And so the chapters that follow aim to identify those territories where solitude thrives. They map out fenceless places worth safeguarding.

Part II

Bolt from the Blue

One can be instructed in society, one is inspired only in solitude.

—*Johann Wolfgang von Goethe*

3

The Wandering Mind

"I'm sorry, Julie, but it's just a fact—people are *terrified* of being in their heads. I read this study where subjects chose to give themselves *electric shocks* rather than be alone with their own thoughts."

It's the summer of 2015 and the University of British Columbia's half-vacated grounds droop with bloom. Julie—an old friend I've run into on campus—gives me a skeptical side-eye and says she's perfectly capable of being alone with her thoughts. Proving her point, she wanders out of the rose garden in search of caffeine. I glower at the plants.

The study was a real one. It was published in 2014 in *Science* and was authored by University of Virginia professor Timothy D. Wilson and his team.[38] Their research revealed that, left to our own company, most of us start to lose it after six to fifteen minutes. The shocks are preferable, despite the pain, because anything—*anything*—is better than what the human brain starts getting up to when left to its own devices.

45

Or so we assume.

What the brain in fact gets up to in the absence of antagonizing external stimuli (buzzing phones, chirping people) is daydreaming. I am purposefully making it sound benign. *Daydreaming* is such a soft term. And yet it refers to a state of mind that most of us—myself included—have learned to suppress like a dirty thought. Perhaps we suppress it out of fear that daydreaming is related to the sin of idle hands. From at least medieval times onward there's been a steady campaign against idleness, that instigator of evil.

Today, in the spaces where I used to daydream, those interstitial moments on a bus, in the shower, or out on a walk, I'm hounded by a guilt and quiet desperation—a panicked need to block my mind from wandering too long on its own. Surely I should be getting something done, making a list of books to read, tabulating (again) the outrageous down payment for our imaginary mortgage. Is it leftover scraps from the Protestant work ethic that nag me so? Samuel Johnson summed things up nicely when he closed a letter to James Boswell, in the fall of 1779, with a motto for modernity: "If you are idle, be not solitary; if you are solitary, be not idle."[39] The mind must be put to use.

I've come to UBC to ask if daydreaming matters, and why. The campus is home to the impressively titled Cognitive Neuroscience of Thought Laboratory, and one of their specialties is "undirected thought processes"—which is shop talk for daydreaming and mind wandering.

Their research is fuelled by volunteers who subject themselves to fMRI brain scans mid-daydream. Today's brain—let's

46

call her Haley—arrives and is promptly asked whether she has any metal in her body (MRI machines are, among other things, enormously powerful magnets). She reports that she's metal-free and so is handed a pair of earplugs—things are going to get frighteningly loud.

Haley is positioned on the sliding bed and the technologist fits a "birdcage" over her head. (Cancer movies don't show the birdcage because it would keep us from seeing the actor's weeping face.) It's the birdcage that actually does the scanning—the giant grey doughnut she's now being slid into is only needed to create a uniform magnetic field; it's the brain's deviations from that field that the birdcage maps.

When the technologist turns on the scanner, it is deafening; a jackhammer effect so powerful that Haley will later report the sound waves were actually tactile. And that's not all she feels. As her head is scanned she feels a calm tingling sensation throughout her body. It's not quantifiable but, like several other study participants, Haley will feel strangely calm after her scan, as though the magnetic field has righted minute disturbances in her body. Eventually her mind grows accustomed to the noise and does what any mind without new stimuli will do—it wanders. Her daydreaming moments are plotted and the data takes six hours to process. (Those instant images in cancer movies are another fib.) But then, bingo. There it is—all angry, nesting smears of light. A portrait of a daydream, in electric blue and red.

Ultimately, such images give us only a very raw notion of what's happening in the mind of a daydreamer. Despite the ninety-minute session's $900 price tag, what it produces is a child's drawing, a base attempt to represent the dance of eighty-six billion neurons. (If I showed you a brain scan from a besotted person or a terrified one, what would you really learn about love or fear?) A floppy-haired PhD student called Matt Dixon describes it to me this way: "You know, it's like we're getting a distant snapshot of something—it's real but it's fuzzy. In this image, we see what's happening in the brain every two seconds, but the brain is actually changing every hundredth of a millisecond. So, yeah, it's a very coarse view. It's valid . . . but it's coarse."

We do get some telling intimations. We now know that when the brain drops its focus on the outside world but remains awake and alert (in other words, when it begins to daydream), it activates something called the default mode network, or DMN. The default mode is anything but a comatose experience. A review of research on the DMN led by Mary Helen Immordino-Yang at the University of Southern California found that a particular style of neural processing is suppressed when we pay direct attention to things, and it emerges when the brain switches to default mode. This daydreaming DMN activity processes personal memories and leads to identity formation.[40]

What exactly are these busy machinations in a "blank" brain? They are several. For starters: a medial temporal subsystem bends memories into mental scenes; a dorsal medial subsystem infers the mental state of others and evaluates one's own; and both the anterior medial prefrontal cortex and posterior cingulate cortex seem to construct personal meaning from external and internal sources. The first meta-analysis of DMN scans (compiled in 2015) found that significant clusters of brain activity outside the DMN were also activated.[41] In sum, daydreaming constitutes an intense and heterogeneous set of brain functions.

Yet this industrious activity plays out while the conscious mind remains utterly unaware of the work—so our thoughts (sometimes really *great* thoughts) emerge without our anticipation or understanding. They emerge from the blue. Daydreaming thoughts may look like "pointless fantasizing" or "complex planning" or "the generation of creative ideas." But, whatever their utility, they arrive unbidden. You could call it an involuntary process, like the pumping of a heart.

After the conscious mind hands over its controls, the brain remains supremely active, all on its own—one of its greatest tricks is the "blank" image it projects to us—a velvet curtain to ward off the interfering ego; a tinted screen to subdue the backseat driver called "I." Our brains are then free to "wander"—which is to say, they're free to do some of their most intensive work.

Studying spontaneous thought and mind wandering was unpopular when the UBC lab's founder, Kalina Christoff, was a student. And she still sees the work of her peers biased against it: "Our culture puts a premium on control in all things," she tells me.

"A lack of control is considered inferior, and so thinking that is uncontrolled becomes suspect. I think it goes back to this very basic idea that order comes from God and the instinctual comes from the devil. I believe that bias spills over into science."

Those idle hands again.

Christoff is a petite woman with a calm gaze to match her methodic voice—she has needed such sureness. Even as an undergrad her interests diverged from others'. While her peers wanted to study analytical thought, she preferred to give people "insight problems"—problems with no clear answer— which required an "aha moment" in order to be solved. A participant might, for example, be given a glass tube with a ball of wax lodged inside; Christoff could hand her a pile of objects and tell her to remove the wax without breaking the glass. The participant must "aha" herself to an answer by arriving at a fresh use for a paper clip or a scrap of paper. Christoff loved to watch for those epiphanies—which she didn't need an MRI machine to witness. "What impressed me was the complete lack of traditional logic as people wandered toward their solutions," she tells me. Mind wandering was managing more than personal memories and a sense of self. The wandering mind was also solving problems in the real world.

We tend to think of problem solving as the implementation of logical steps toward an answer that is predetermined and inevitable. In this way we assert control over things. But Christoff found that her insight problems were being solved, instead, by a process of association that was actually very poetic. The solutions participants arrived at could never have been deduced via strict logic. (Rebus puzzles are common examples of insight problems. E.g., What is meant by "sta4nce"? Answer: "For instance.") Christoff found that hardly anyone around her was interested in this dark space of human ingenuity. "It was uncharted territory."

After a PhD at Stanford and postdoc work at Cambridge, Christoff went to UBC and founded her lab. As the initial brain-scan data flooded in, it made her imagine the mind as a sort of muscle system that relied on opposing forces. To bend your arm, for example, you flex one muscle while relaxing another—straightening your arm requires the reverse. Similarly, Christoff's new vision of a well-tuned mind included an interplay between concentration and stream of consciousness. Over-exercise one or the other and you impair the functioning of the whole apparatus. "In our culture we're always encouraged to practise concentrating," she tells me, "but we're discouraged from the wide-ranging modes of thought we experience in solitude."

Given enough solitude and enough time, the mind shifts into default mode and pans through connections that at first seem wholly random. It explores problems with a curiosity and openness we might never choose to entertain. But this randomness is crucial. "The power of the wandering mind," says Christoff, "is precisely the fact that it censors nothing. It can make connections you would never otherwise make." Daydreaming is an inherently creative process, she says, because the daydreamer is open to bizarre new options. Fresh insights and methods that don't already exist in the larger culture are revealed through this solitary style of brainwork. By contrast, analytical thinking, logical thinking, is all about the exclusion and critiquing of ideas so that the brain can become a guided laser that operates with surgical precision. The conscious, analytical style of thinking that our schools train us to use always silences the bizarre or unpopular ideas that the daydreaming mind might try on. "Analytical thinking is ideal for weighing options in a well-defined problem," says Christoff. But that power is also its weakness, she says: "Analytical thinking is antithetical to inspiration."

Albert Einstein famously noticed this separation of duties in the mind. His attitude toward that difference was paraphrased by Bob Samples: "The intuitive mind is a sacred gift and the rational mind is a faithful servant. We have created a society that honours the servant and has forgotten the gift."[42] Einstein believed that the daydreaming mind's ability to link things is, in fact, our only path toward fresh ideas. There is a kind of assembly line, one could argue, with knowledge and conversation pouring in at the start and, later down the track, a stretch of silence and daydreaming. Both ends of the factory are necessary to produce the crucial product—the insight.

Isaac Newton laboured over his own research in almost complete isolation. A lonely childhood gave way to a disaffected time at Cambridge, where absurd Aristotelian physics was still being taught. But then, in 1665, the plague struck Cambridge and—in perhaps the only wonderful thing to come of that disaster—Newton was obliged to retreat to the isolation of his family's farmhouse in Woolsthorpe. It was there, forcibly removed from the university's community, that Newton discovered the laws of motion and gravity. It was there, in a garden and not in a lecture hall, that he saw a falling apple and wondered why.

Physicists like Einstein and Newton are among our most fundamental thinkers, and they were particularly aware of what solitude brings to serious thought. Felicity Mellor, a researcher at Imperial College London, criticizes the new generation of advanced study institutes for emphasizing collaboration and social atmospheres at the expense of such solitary contemplation. The institutions Mellor studies exhibit what she calls a "near-exclusive focus" on communication between scholars and, in their own words, call for "international engagement" and "collaborative research projects." The Francis Crick Institute, in London, which opened in 2016, is a paradigmatic example: it's designed with open-plan labs and glass walls to ensure collaboration. The institute's strategy document cheers how "scientists will be drawn together at interaction and collaboration facilities located at the centre of each floor."

"The need for periods of withdrawal and solitude," Mellor writes, "are no longer acknowledged as a means of facilitating intellectual advances." Although every fundamental shift in physics has required a good dose of solitude, "reticence and silence seem to have no place in the modern research agenda."[43] Peter Higgs, the Nobel Prize–winning godfather of the Hadron Collider, backs Mellor up, saying his trailblazing work would be impossible today because the peace and solitude he enjoyed in the 1960s has vanished.[44] We can only imagine how premature sharing could deflate a unified field theory or mangle an explanation for the origination of gamma ray bursts.

What is true for institutions is also true for individuals. We all have daily proof that moments of aloneness allow for the drifting, unfocused mind to be inspired. Like others, I'm hit by my better ideas first thing in the morning, even lying in bed, before the world has poured any noise or hassle onto me. A novel thought might strike me in the shower, or while I'm drinking my coffee and fuzzily apprehending the patterns of birds outside. Almost all my writer friends swear by early-morning writing. And the psychiatrist Anthony Storr found the same, saying that "by far the greater number of new ideas occur during a state of reverie, intermediate between waking and sleeping."[45] It's as though the brain is allowed to have its genius moment before our lumbering, bureaucratic *idea of thinking* puts on a tie and gets in the way.

As we continue to chat about all this, Christoff moves toward surprisingly philosophical places: "If our mode of life leaves us feeling empty sometimes," she tells me, "it may be because we aren't left to our own devices, we aren't allowed to mull things over. We're deprived of that sense of meaning and happiness that mind wandering can produce." An extended stare out the rain-smeared window may be as key to consolidating our thoughts as REM sleep.

Alison Gopnik, the acclaimed psychology professor at the University of California–Berkley, has pushed this notion even further. She argues that the rush of pleasure we get from an "aha moment" is the equivalent of an orgasm for the thinking mind.[46] The pleasure of an orgasm, after all, is just a motivating bit of trickery that our bodies employ to make sure we procreate;* similarly, the pleasure of an "aha" may be built into our DNA to ensure that we learn more about the world. This is a deeply encouraging thought. If we've evolved to take great pleasure from the moment when fresh connections are forged, then letting our mind wander is no longer a guilty indulgence—it is crucial to our success and survival. Our blueprint demands it.

I walk out into startling daylight and sneeze. My medial temporal lobe produces a spontaneous thought, but then my fronto-parietal control network seizes on the thought and derails the daydreaming process, focusing my mind on this one, crucial notion: *Where can I get a decent snack around here?*

Twenty minutes later, sated, I decide to give myself a good three hours of practice in mind wandering. I so seldom drift for that length of time, and Christoff has made me worry my brain is starved for it. She made the point that there is daydreaming and then there is *daydreaming*: a frantic, distracted mind may be broadly characterized as "wandering," but one requires a

---

* I am using a heterosexual accent here.

luxury of empty time before the mind can be expected to engender fresh insights. True wandering requires a long leash.

How to begin? The mind wanders best when we're a little bored, so a pointless walk seems smart. I head across the sun-baked campus, going nowhere in particular. Next: silence the digital prompts that will sabotage things. My phone is killed and buried in my back pocket. On the off chance something worthwhile pops up, I allow myself a notebook and pen.

I am miles and miles from home. From friends, too, and (most important) from my nagging laptop. I have, for once, these three sweet hours that are not accounted for. This shining afternoon I am left—precariously—to my own devices. I begin to walk in great gambolling loops around the campus—nowhere, nowhere. And nothing comes.

All I can think about is thought itself: "I'm going to daydream about daydreaming . . . ," says my brain. Then, an unbidden rejoinder: "Now I'm sort of examining my wish to daydream about daydreaming. . . ." This thought, in turn, triggers an anxiety response: "Now I'm *worried* I shouldn't *wish* to daydream about daydreaming. . . ." The hall of mirrors extends for a few more steps before I shake my head. That way lies madness. Or analytical thought, anyway, which I'm trying to avoid. I need to let my mind take the wheel, I need to get out of its way. It's difficult, subtle, like separating a yolk from the egg white in your hand. A deftness is required.

Once the nervous energy burns off, though, my brain settles and—miraculously—it does start scavenging through strange attic boxes.

Freud appears early on (typical): "We may lay it down that a happy person never phantasies, only an unsatisfied one."[47] My head has recalled this sour note from an essay he wrote about creative writers and daydreaming. And I find his point both depressing and true: nobody would produce an alternative to bare reality unless something was found wanting. When Beatrix Potter was a little girl, imagining stories about rabbits that wear smart jackets, she was a lonely child who needed to concoct some company. And when Monet painted his impressionistic water lilies, he was a man deeply dissatisfied with traditional views of nature. The inventions of writers and artists are forged through dissatisfaction. That discrepancy between the world we walk through and the world inside of us encourages some to try to build a bridge (in the shape of a book about talking bunnies or an impressionistic painting). A perfectly happy artist would be a failure.

No, I think, blinking at the wooded trail I've wandered onto, the daydreamer cannot be wholly satisfied. But what else? These three empty hours are a crazy luxury, and I realize not everyone can easily access such blank space. Virginia Woolf said as much in *A Room of One's Own*: there would have been many more great female authors had women been given some peace and quiet to wander in. She hopes that female writers—historically forced to cram a line in here or there between the pressures of society and children—will soon be able to "idle" and to "loiter at street corners and let the line of thought dip deep into the stream."[48] The *right* to separate must be won before we arrive at that "state of reverie" Storr describes, in which "the greater number of new ideas occur."[49]

From my writer's brain come several examples of scribes who safeguarded their rambling detachment. The names of poets come first: Wordsworth, Byron, Plath, Sarton—they all wandered away, whether by retreating to a cottage in the Lake District or by more ornery means. Rilke sums up their strategy in one of his famous letters: "love your solitude and try to sing out with the pain it causes you."[50]

I've trailed down to the shore—to the nudist beach on the campus's western perimeter. A man is swimming through copper-gilt sunset-waves, alone and naked and heading toward no destination. The pattern of his arms draws my attention long enough for something to fall over in my head—strange: it's Kafka. I recall that Franz Kafka was very direct about his need for isolated daydreaming: "Writing is utter solitude, the descent into the cold abyss of oneself." Was it the cold water that reminded me? There's a story about Kafka's fiancée, Felice Bauer, who announced that she'd like to sit beside him while he wrote. He sent her a letter saying her presence would destroy his work. "One can never be alone enough when one writes," he told her. "There can never be enough silence . . . even night is not night enough."[51] They called off the wedding.

These scraps swirl inside my head a half-hour later as I poke back up the trail toward campus. I imagine my random thoughts are like bits of loose genetic material in some primordial puddle—combining, recombining, stealing protein-sized notions from one another. They evolve into slightly altered thoughts that are better suited to their unique environment—which is to say, my mind.

It's only three hours of my life—and perhaps I haven't arrived at anything particularly shattering, no real eureka. And still, I'm struck by how wholly necessary the wandering mind is to insight. We cannot compound the ideas of others into a singular meaning for ourselves unless we're given a private mental workshop in which to hammer at them. (Will I ever be able to write my book, I worry, if I can't build such a workshop for myself?) Without daydreams our minds are only parrots—or, worse, computers. Daydreams are the engineers of new worlds.

And yet I realize that all I've really "invented" this afternoon are new pathways, new networks, new patterns of thought in my own cloistered mind—as a whole, my daydreaming remains impractical and fuzzy. Why did I think of Freud? Why did I think of Kafka? And what about the hundreds of bits of brain-flotsam that I immediately forgot or couldn't put down in words? The process looks nothing like the Cartesian vision of the mind we're sometimes fed—with the little man, my "self," rational and purposeful, at the helm of the brain, guiding me toward a sublime conclusion. Instead, the brain of a daydreamer does not much care whether it *arrives* anywhere at all. That is its luxury, and also its value. It wanders down the aisles of an endless library, slaps a hand along the spines of books like a child.

The light is failing. The campus feels suddenly desolate, and my daydreaming lands on an image of old Archimedes—

naked and running through the streets of Athens, shouting his famous "Eureka!" (Was it the naked swimmer who brought the bathtub scene, the poster boy of solitary daydreaming, to mind?) Archimedes solved the mystery of buoyancy in a flash, leaping from his tub with the force of it all. But perhaps daydreaming isn't really about "eureka" moments after all. The truth is that most of our daydreams are not particularly noble or important or fruitful. Our curiosity trails down avenues and culs-de-sac with shameless promiscuity.

I shiver. Things have turned, suddenly, to a cool and leafy dusk. My feet turn toward the bus stop, and I'm wondering, wandering still.

Sadly, eureka-level daydreams are not handed out to just anyone who wanders through the woods. An annoying truth about daydreaming is that it takes practice to get good at it. And we are sorely out of practice. Do we even notice anymore that there are qualitative differences in the way we spend our free time? That an hour's reverie in the park is not the same as an hour spent chasing Pokémon? When Bertrand Russell wrote "In Praise of Idleness" he noted, "The wise use of leisure, it must be conceded, is a product of civilization and education."[52] This notion that there is a "wise use of leisure" may be a surprise to us.

Pulitzer Prize–winning author Sebastian de Grazia believes the wise use of "spare" time is not just a product of civilization but a litmus test for that civilization's success. He writes: "Perhaps you can judge the inner health of a land by the capacity of its people to do nothing—to lie abed musing, to amble about aimlessly, to sit having coffee—because whoever can do nothing, letting his thoughts go where they may, must be at peace with himself."[53]

These words make me think of men in linen shirts outside brasseries, smoking and staring at cobblestones; they make me think of women in floppy hats, eating gelato and shuffling down rainy beaches in Puerto Rico. By de Grazia's standard, daydreaming ought to be placed on the Quality of Life Index alongside rates of literacy. By his standard, things in our busy world start to look impoverished, starved.

Meanwhile, I start to see time-devouring apps like Candy Crush as pacifiers for a culture unwilling or unable to experience a finer, adult form of leisure. We believed those who told us that the devil loves idle hands. And so we gave our hands over for safekeeping. We long for constant proof of our effectiveness, our accomplishments. And perhaps it's this longing for proof, for glittering external validation, that makes our solitude so vulnerable to those who would harvest it.

4

Daydream Destroyers

On the subway I was sandwiched by two large men in matching navy suits. Each was studiously curled over a game of Candy Crush. I suppose I might have used those few spare minutes to amble through the curious glades of my imagination but, instead, affecting anthropological duty, I gave up my own daydreaming time in order to glance back and forth at their sparkling phones. We swayed as a set, the three of us, with the car's rhythmic rocking, and the Candy Crush candies rained down endlessly into the gnarled hands of these middle-aged men. Silently I coached them: good move, bad move, good move. . . .

The premise of Candy Crush is simple in the extreme: various tempting candies appear in a miniature grid on the screen; the player swaps their order to make a row of matching sweets. This set then glimmers and disappears, creating a cascade effect as the candies above tumble down to form endless new arrangements.

The game's creator, King Digital Entertainment, enjoyed 1.6 billion daily game plays in the first quarter of 2015. Tech bloggers were stunned to discover Candy Crush was making more money than all Nintendo games combined. Indeed, in-app purchases and other revenue streams at King became so attractive that the company was purchased by Activision Blizzard (makers of the *Call of Duty* and *Warcraft* series) for $5.9 billion in 2015.[54] How did such a basic premise prompt such deeply addictive behaviour? It's about more than our addiction to sugar, though the candy shapes are no more an accident than the cherry and watermelon icons that appear on the spinning wheels of a casino's slot machine. Something primal seems to be triggered by those raining candies. The truth is, we don't play Candy Crush so much as get played.

One reason is ludic loops. These are short cycles of repeated actions that cater to our id, and to a brute, reptilian desire for play (as opposed to more developed, narrative-driven ideas of play that have coherent beginnings and endings). Behavioural psychologists have found that we fall into these miniature, repeating loops of pleasure and are driven to access that pleasure again, again, again, without wondering when it will end. Even the faintest of dopamine hits will work. The discovery of repeating patterns works well—humans are hard-wired to enjoy finding patterns. (This is why babies so adore their building blocks and also why many slot-machine gamblers stop only when their bladders force the issue.) This instinct is reinforced on Candy Crush, where the discovery of a pattern—a simple row of candies—results in an outsized

celebration. The game cheers "Sweet!" or "Tasty!" and show-
ers the user with points. Not just *a* point, of course, but dozens
or hundreds at a time.

When I found myself flanked by those gaming business-
men—and then found myself equally entranced—ludic loops
were spinning us into what's become known as "the machine
zone." Natasha Dow Schüll, a cultural anthropologist at MIT,
has devoted years to studying this entranced state. "In the
machine zone," she told me, "people will stand in rising flood
waters or amidst a deafening alarm, and they will *keep on
going*." Those are examples from her research, by the way, not
hyperbole. For a person who has fallen into the machine zone,

> a tunnel vision occurs where you actually lose a sense
> of the body. Physical pain can even disappear. You feel
> connected to the machine, almost as though you're
> merging with it. And I don't mean just your hands at
> the controls, but a merging of your intentions with the
> intentions of the program. There's not really a *you*
> anymore. The self has fallen away.[55]

A person in the machine zone, then, is alone with the
machine and yet not in a solitary state. If it were solitude,
there'd be a rich engagement; instead, a person in the machine
zone has abandoned engagement entirely. What apps like
Candy Crush are best at is demolishing solitude. Put another
way, they're an invasive species, *dominating* the ground where
solitude would otherwise grow.

Schüll discovered the machine zone while studying hard-core slot-machine gamblers at casinos. Today, however, the zone notion has crept into conversations about gaming and social apps. "There is a kinship between gambling and the apps on our phones," she told me, adding, "I've increasingly seen a convergence of technology and gambling." Her words struck me forcibly.

The difference between technology and gambling, though, is that Silicon Valley is able to talk quite openly about "addictive" technologies and can even foster a cottage industry of "behaviour design specialists" who guide their creation, whereas if casinos were caught taking either approach they would be painted as villains. We know to frown at the addictiveness of gambling, yet we're impressed at the business acumen of those who design addictive technologies. We fail to recognize that the latter are taking their cues from the former. And by making a science of distraction, Silicon Valley can ultimately be far more effective than Las Vegas, for Silicon Valley has machine learning and adaptive algorithms on its side. This convergence of tech and gambling fills our lives with ludic loops and the machine zone's soporific fog.

The result is less space for sustained daydreaming, for a mind in the machine zone never wanders at all—it is ruthlessly tethered. And, whereas a daydreaming mind is powerfully awake, a mind in the machine zone only drifts in a soft, pseudo-slumber.

Candy Crush and the next generation of ludic loop apps, then, tug users toward an anti-solitude. The player may appear alone, but (as with the slot-machine gambler) the richness and openness of solitude have been rubbed out by the strict pleasure-seeking bias of the game's design—a bias that tilts toward a kind of nihilism. Schüll told me that there is no real goal when one is in the machine zone. When we read reports about teenage boys in China who wear diapers while playing online games so they won't miss a minute of the action, we may well question their sanity, and the sanity of their idea of "progress." The boy stares; he feels as though he's building something, gaining something, but the real point is the ludic loop itself. The point of the system is more system.

Those ludic loops can be harnessed for uses besides mere addiction for its own sake. Those who engineer ludic loops are better able to process solitude into corporate gains. By inserting busyness into previously solitary moments, tech companies create "value" out of thin air.

It's easy and it happens all the time. From 2006 to 2011, for example, Google ran an online "game" called Google Image Labeler (yay, image labelling!). Players were shown a random image and asked to tag it with as many labels as they could; when their tags matched the tag suggested by another player, both players gained points. Quick, impulsive actions led to a never-ending cascade of positive feedback, not unlike a slot machine's reward system. And the data banks of Google Image won a pile of free labour—players as unpaid workers, building a more useful search engine that Google could then monetize. All Google had to do was set up a ludic loop, and basic human drives took care of the rest.

What might this look like in 2041? Let's pop into the future. . . . Samuel Flores is a digital serf by his own choosing—or that's what his parents tell their friends. He's thirty-three years old and, each morning, he slinks out of the basement suite at his mom's house and goes to the park with his tablet. There he puts in a solid six hours of labour-gaming, mostly liking and sharing promoted content in order to earn points from blue-chip corporations. Unlike old-fashioned click farms in India—where thousands of factory-style workers would "like" content or "follow" paying customers—Samuel is one of millions of "untethered" click workers; they are paid not with cash but with followers of their own. Samuel's pretty sure most of them are bots, but it hardly seems to matter. It's light and constant work, and he is both addicted and dedicated to the boosts he's been earning. He believes in his future; he believes he won't always be a serf. But he hasn't had time just yet to plan what that future might look like. He is building a brand that will be big enough to free him one day. And he can eat his mom's macaroni until then.

To a media baron hunting for short-term profits, a daydreaming mind must look like an awful waste. All that time and attention left to wander, directionless! Making use of the blank spaces in a person's life—draining the well of reverie— has become one of the missions of modernity.

This stems back to the late sixteenth century, when Western civilization grew increasingly fond of exactitude: dates, distances, rates—it was the measuring of life that girded our new rationalism. And nowhere is this more clear than in the management of time. It was in that century that clocks became domestic—meaning they appeared in ordinary homes. As though in sympathy, time-saving devices proliferated. The next two centuries saw the invention of plowing machines, adding machines, the fountain pen, the threshing machine, the power loom, the sewing machine, the typewriter, the steamboat, all of which served a single great goal—live faster.

This impulse to measure and maximize time became ubiquitous—and personal—as the industrial age bloomed in the nineteenth century: workers were coordinated, their movements and schedules parsed by the implementation of clocks, whistles, and factory bells. Mechanical timekeeping brought workers in line with an unyielding efficiency. This steady rationalizing of the workforce culminated at the tail of the nineteenth century with the arrival of Taylorism (a.k.a. scientific management), which ruthlessly streamlined workforces, going so far as to dictate the physical movement of workers, making them almost literal cogs; Frederick Taylor's theories later inspired Henry Ford's famously efficient production lines.

In the 1880s, the electric elevator and the steel-frame skyscraper it would ride did their part to radically reorganize the workforce—we were slotted upward into increasingly rarefied and abstracted environments. This was the new reality that inspired Fritz Lang to create his fantasy *Metropolis*, in which pale, synchronized workers trudge to their soulless jobs. And this was the reality Aldous Huxley confronted when he declared—in his foreword to *Brave New World*—that "in an age of advanced technology, inefficiency is the sin against the Holy Ghost."[56]

By the 1950s, that war against blank space was exemplified by the figure of super-achieving Dick Tracy with his radio watch. Tracy is always connected, always getting things done. (There's not a moment to lose!) This fantasy of tech-enabled effectiveness was so attractive that Seico and Linux both announced similar phone watches for executives in the 1980s and '90s, long before any software could match the reach of an executive's ambition.

The connectivity arms race had its tipping point in 1998, when a smallish company in Waterloo, Canada, called Research In Motion introduced the first device capable of mobile access to email: the BlackBerry. The days of clumsy pagers came to a swift end. From then on conversations would be wireless, mobile, and constant—from the singular BlackBerry came a movable feast. BlackBerrys were originally geared toward a class of bullish American executives—people who not only prided themselves on being indispensable but had a latent addiction to connection that no technology had yet tapped. The fantasy of every CEO, of course, is to be an octopus, reaching out in multiple directions at once. In 1998, BlackBerry was the closest thing.

Today, wearable technology like the Apple Watch handily outstrips those earlier efforts. A level of executive function that began as a "superhero" signifier (Dick Tracy gear) had first morphed into a "businessman" necessity, and finally became the base level of busyness for everyday folk. We are all Dick Tracy now.

The promise of becoming a superhero (or at least a moderately improved human) tempts us down the path, away from our daydreaming selves. The promise goes like this: attend to this tool and you will be smarter, you will be more effective, you will wield more agency and influence more people than you ever could have done on your own.

Our technologies convince us that solitary thinking is worthless—what a useless idiot I would be on my own! We are convinced that our brainwork can only be improved by these interjections, that technologies designed to destroy solitude must be here to enlighten and empower us. Whether we're playing Candy Crush or tweeting at Donald Trump, that sense of heightened agency is always there. We weld the isolated human mind to technologies designed to shepherd us toward more productive pastures while forgetting that disconnected thinking has its own merits.

Former *Wired* editor Clive Thompson argues in his book *Smarter Than You Think* that the Internet allows us to become "centaurs"—we enjoy a hybrid state in which we achieve ESP-level ambient awareness of friends and coworkers. We become, in Thompson's words, "conversational thinkers." And he believes "we're augmenting ourselves" when we become these centaurs.[57] It's an attractive argument. And it would be churlish not to grant that new tech can hack out startling new paths of inquiry. The emergence of big data analytics alone has provided enormous boons to the way hospitals understand their patients, the way governments respond to citizens, and the way academics burrow into archives.

But thinking online makes you at once the smartest and the dumbest person in the room. I'll sometimes indulge in a kind of tandem-talk, cruising the Internet for supportive information while chatting on the phone. "Jeez," my friend eventually says. "You know *a lot* about sea monkeys." And how many times have I worked myself into a frenzy of online thinking, with ten tabs open on my browser and snatches of input taken from this journal or that newspaper as I try to collage my way toward a single vision? It's the mental equivalent of running with a jetpack.

Each time I lay my hands on a computer's keyboard, I'm tempted. Think of the glacial progress of quills and pens across a page . . . how stunted that mode of thought-processing feels compared with the keyboard writer's racing progress. Think how dull pencil marks are when compared with the literal illumination of text that the poorest computer user enjoys. It's easy to believe that the miracle of the machinery—its fascinating *effectiveness*, its sanitized lines of crisply formed Times New Roman letters—must be making what we write, and therefore what we *think*, somehow stronger.

Of course, we began pining for this mind meld with our technology many years before the advent of the Internet. The desire became obvious in the summer of 1945, when an MIT engineering professor called Vannevar Bush asked what American scientists ought to focus their energies on, now that World War Two had concluded. Bush—a forthright and brilliant man—was uniquely positioned to ask the question; he had served as director of the Office of Scientific Research and Development during the war, marshalling six thousand scientists toward some of the greatest militaristic goals in history. Come peacetime, Bush's interests swerved toward more humane ends. His new call to arms was capsulized in a seminal essay titled "As We May Think," which was published in the *Atlantic Monthly* that July.[58] In it, Bush imagines something called the Memex, which is as close as anyone in the 1940s got to imagining the Internet. He sees it in "centaur" terms: it would be "a sort of mechanized private file and library," he writes. "A Memex is a device in which an individual stores all his books, records, and communications, and which is mechanized so that it may be consulted with exceeding speed and flexibility. It is an enlarged intimate supplement to his memory." It would look, roughly, like a desk, with a keyboard and a set of buttons and levers—Bush probably imagined something we would call *very Jetsons*.

This compact bearer of world knowledge would provide new ways of learning, and we would discover new forms of creativity. New strategies for learning and thinking are, in fact, imperative for modern man, Bush realizes: "He has built a civilization so complex that he needs to mechanize his records more fully if he is to push his experiment to its logical conclusion and not merely become bogged down part way there by overtaxing his limited memory." Flooded by data—by the very Niagara of data that the twentieth century produced—humans suddenly needed an aide, some portal through which to manage it all, make it useful. Our minds could no longer *work* on their own.

Crucially, Bush also imagined that the data stored in one's Memex could be transferred and shared with others. "Wholly new forms of encyclopedias will appear," he wrote (shades of *Wikipedia*). "The lawyer has at his touch the associated opinions and decisions of his whole experience, and of the experience of friends and authorities."

Bush could not have guessed, while imagining this charming data salon, the creeping influence of social platform technologies. Seventy years later, though, it's become clear that nothing can grow strong online without losing its seclusion. That Memex mind, that tech-boosted mind, is always in danger of becoming a hive mind. By necessity, it bends toward sharing with a constant solicitude.

Meanwhile, we often forget to distinguish between what the Memex is good at and what *we* are good at. Our computers will not daydream for us. Ada Lovelace (daughter of Lord Byron) was the first to point this out, back in 1842. Writing about the first conceptualized computer—Charles Babbage's Analytical Engine—Lovelace found it necessary to explain, in what became the ur-text of computer theory, that the proposed contraption was not a "thinking" machine. She understood that the machine, which could calculate complex math problems, was being mistaken for a mind. And so she writes, "The Analytical Engine has no pretensions to *originate* anything. It can do *whatever we know how to order it* to perform." *No pretensions to originate anything.* Lovelace seems to foreshadow the disdain of Pablo Picasso, who famously mumbled that computers didn't much excite him since "they can only give you answers."

What's at risk is our ability to turn the meandering mind toward a proper, patient reverie—to steer our drifting curiosity away from digital titillation, away from addictive, nihilistic ludic loops and the attractions of sociability, toward a solitude where it could—who knows?—stumble upon uncharted territory.

We can easily intuit how daydreaming is key to the poet's progress, or how locking the door against the world is a necessary step for frizzy-haired professors of quantum mechanics. But too often we assume that bouts of sustained daydreaming are not for us ordinary folk. Too often we allow ourselves to be absorbed, instead, by anxious preoccupations that have been fed to us by others.

Choosing a mental solitude, then, is a disruptive act, a true sabotage of the schemes of ludic loop engineers and social media barons. Choosing solitude is a gorgeous waste.

By chance, I came across Dante Gabriel Rossetti's 1880 painting, *The Day Dream*, while working on these pages and thought—*this person gets it*. Jane Morris, wife of the designer William Morris, is shown sitting in a sycamore tree, a forgotten book in her lap. A flower (honeysuckle) has fallen from her hand onto those abandoned pages. And the woman herself—proud and pale, in full Pre-Raphaelite glory—stares out-of-frame, lost to her reverie. Her expression is profoundly blank; the viewer may wonder at but never grasp her state of mind. "Tow'rd deep skies" are "not deeper than her look," wrote Rossetti in an accompanying poem.[59]

The daydreamer is like the tree in which she crouches, oblivious to the red-faced plans of industry. It's understood that if someone were to come along and put her mind "to use," she would gain little from the interruption.

Rossetti did not have fMRI brain scans. He did not have the research of psychoanalysts, nor data records from Facebook to sift through. But he knew. He knew enough to prize the daydreamer sitting in her sycamore. To prize the daydreamer and leave her be.

As for myself, I began to see that coming to terms with my solitude would demand much more than the occasional daydreaming session. Those morsels only whetted my appetite—I wanted more. I wanted to draw bolder lines around myself. But doing that meant figuring out who I really was. Where, after all, does the crowd end and where do I begin?

Part III

Who Do You Think You Are?

Beauty begins the moment you decide to be yourself.

—*Coco Chanel*

5

Style

One fine afternoon at the fall end of 1924, a man made his way down Rosebery Avenue, in London, and passersby whipped around to stare. His arms were shackled with coral and topaz jewellery, which clattered as he walked, for his hands were convulsed by a perpetual flutter. His face, nearly orange from powder, was punctuated with vermillion lips and an eye shadow that young ladies didn't dare to wear. Thanks to endless pots of henna, his head was topped with a frizz of crimson hair, which teetered hazardously to and fro as he minced along the pavement. The man gossiped, momentarily, with a friend heading the other way, and the voice that emerged was as shocking as the body: each word seemed to insinuate and divulge rather than flatly *say*.

Around the corner, an idle gang of men came after him. He tried to hurry away but they followed—hungry for sport—and someone sneered, "Who the hell do you think you are?"

One grabbed at his throat, another at his crotch, and another at both. Their pack-like confidence grew as each snap went unpunished. When he went so far as to address one of them as "sir," the beating began. He was knocked to the ground, where he struggled to protect his face from their fists and feet. He managed to leap into a passing cab, but they dragged him out and knocked him on his back. Finally, the man pulled himself up against the facade of Finsbury Town Hall and said to his assailants, "I seem to have annoyed you gentlemen in some way."[60] The lynch mob, overcome with laughter, dispersed.

This was a fairly ordinary event in the life of Quentin Crisp. The violence of his attackers never surprised him (he was raised on violence); rather, what surprised him that afternoon was that he was once again left alive.

Homosexual acts were still illegal in England in the 1920s, and Crisp (a committed homosexual) understood this to mean that his very existence was criminal. It did not follow, however, that he would hide. Society could make Crisp an outsider but it could not undo him. So, at a time when the vast majority of gay men and women lived in torturous secrecy, Crisp flagrantly advertised himself in the street, and was regularly beaten for his trouble.

None of this abuse deterred Crisp. Which raises the question: why would a man choose to invite violence when it would be so simple to scrub off the makeup and train himself to ape the walk and manners of his fellow Englishmen? Why make things so difficult? The lipstick, the jewellery, all his exaggerated, camping ways—the determined *style* of his existence—was a deeply political act. Many years later, after his memoir of that time had become a bestseller, after he had dubbed himself "one of the stately homos of England," after he had moved to New York, where taxi drivers gave him free rides in exchange for autographs and David Letterman laughed with him on television, Crisp explained his flagrant expression of personal style this way: "When you'd see me walking along Fulham Road, you'd think, 'There's one. Doesn't seem to be doing any harm, does he?' And you'd think, 'They must have a life. They can't always be in drag, in clubs. They must live.'"[61]

They must live. This seems, to me, like the single most salient reason for individual style: we are telling each other that, buried beneath all the common trappings of culture, we are here, and we are human, and we are not to be washed away in a morass of conformity. In this way, what counts as "human" may grow a little.

The biographer Michael Holroyd wrote that Crisp "stands for postjudice versus prejudice."[62] In other words, Crisp saw that prepared ideas and opinions should always be suspect, that one should develop one's own ideas and sensibilities at any cost. Crisp saw that the bravery to be undeniably one's self can be a revolutionary act. To be truly stylish (as opposed to merely "in style," which is the opposite) is to be unabashedly one's self, without reference to the fashions and demands of a sweltering crowd. And this refusal to conform is enormously beneficial to humanity as a whole. When, deep into the more permissive 1960s, Crisp sat down to write his autobiography, he called it *The Naked Civil Servant*. And that is what he was.

To Crisp, the pursuit of a personal style, the warding off of convention, is a good work that we ought to pursue in every corner of our lives:

- When dressing: watch out if "all we know when we see you coming down the street is that you had enough money to buy *Vanity Fair*. We don't know anything about *you*."[63]
- When speaking: avoid jargon and slang, since "someone with style shuns identification with a group."[64]
- When struck by poverty: "your style does not prosper or suffer according to your cash flow."[65]
- When struck by wealth: "it can't buy you style, or intelligence, or beauty, or wit, or affection, or respect" (though "it can definitely buy you happiness").[66]
- When old and broken: remember "a nursing home is nothing more than a club where group dying is practised."[67]

Every hour, argues Crisp, should be shaped by our private considerations and personal attitudes. His example reminds us that each expression is a political expression; we're either insisting on being ourselves or acquiescing to a larger system.

Style, then, is achieved only when we become more like ourselves. Alfred Hitchcock called the effort "self-plagiarism." We work to become who we already are. We brave the threat of obscurity, bristle at the collective force of a platform economy, and enjoy whatever weirdness we can protect inside ourselves.

———

The innocuous-looking smiley emoji might be the greatest threat to Crispian style today. In one of my surreptitious subway-stalking moments, I watched a young woman send a phalanx of them to her friend while maintaining a stone-cold grimace on her actual face. She was neither laughing out loud nor cracking a grin. When she looked up at me I smiled dumbly, and her expression became aggressively blank.

Her being disingenuous is not what bothered me. (Without disingenuous chatter, people would have no friends at all.) What bothered me was that she was being disingenuous with so little effort at *style*. By substituting emojis for emotions, it seemed that she'd sent her voice through some kind of meat grinder and it had come out the other end as personality sausage. (I'm no better: Kenny and I were at a party recently where some well-meaning fellow unlocked the emoji function on both our phones and now all conversation is diminished. I start by trying to explain myself with words but I end up sending Kenny rows of palm trees and panda bears instead.)

Emoticons and emojis scratch out individual voices and offer instead a limited shopping list of feelings. (The improvement is only meagre when the thumbs-up icon becomes available in multiple skin tones.) Not that we ever really took advantage of our language's awesome bounty. There are more than one million words in the English language—indeed, researchers at Harvard and Google have ascertained that we're currently gaining about 8,500 new words each year[68]—but most people employ only 5,000 when they speak and 10,000 when they write. This means we use only 0.5 to 1 per cent of the words at our disposal. (More generous studies put the number as high as 3 per cent.) We tend to use the same words over and over again because we're, of course, exhausted and it's so much easier to speak on autopilot. A friend of mine who does communication workshops with corporate clients tells me this laziness is especially apparent in their culture. At the office, everyone tells everyone that everything is "amazing" and "exciting" until the words have been pounded into a kind of semantic pabulum. Of course they do. The pabulum is safe, inoffensive, a way to groom without taking a stand—or standing out. And so, as we scroll through the available smiley faces and wineglass icons, these shortcuts to sensibility, we seldom stop to wonder whether our solitary voices have been squashed by the predetermined flashcards of sentiment we're encouraged to hold up in their place.

:-)

The first emoticon was a sideways smiley face built from a colon, a hyphen, and a parenthesis. It's a cave drawing compared with today's suite of fully graphic options. (The "smiling pile of poop" icon is particularly popular in my native Canada.) But that first little smiley was a linguistic revolution when it was proposed in 1982.

Computer scientist Scott Fahlman found that Internet message boards were riddled with miscommunications. Irony and sarcasm didn't come across as people tapped out their messages, and this led to needless hurt feelings. Most users, it seemed, had underestimated the amount of information they gathered from facial gestures and tones of voice. So Fahlman, a jolly-looking bear of a man, proposed a solution: tag a smiley on the end of your message and everyone will know you meant well. The bright species of emoji that have since emerged may be the Astroturf of literary expression, but they are also shiny and implacable, incapable of producing offence. We cleave to them because we fear our own voices will get us into trouble. If we use our own words, we fear that the Internet will twist and misrepresent our voice. (More than thirty years after the smiley was invented, happy face and heart emojis still make up more than half of all emojis used. Not dollar signs, not puppies, not beer mugs; our main pictographic concern is that people know our intentions are pleasant.) I doubt it's a coincidence that women use twice as many emojis as men—is it not likely that people used to having their voices institutionally diminished and mangled would be interested in buttressing their messages?

What began as closing punctuation to messages has evolved into a full-on breed of communication—the digital hieroglyph. The most popular emoji by far is "Face with Tears of Joy," which handily replaces the text-based "LOL" and even became the Oxford Dictionaries Word of the Year in 2015. But the digi-glyph language is complex enough that there are also symbols for "Mountain Cableway" and "Moon Viewing Ceremony."

Two friends, Matt Gray and Tom Scott, set up a website in 2014 where people could communicate *only* via emojis—even usernames were strings of emojis. It was a joke, but nonetheless, sixty thousand people signed up; Gray and Scott began taking confused calls from investors who thought their site was an ambitious new tech startup. Meanwhile, a data engineer called Fred Benenson pushed things to nosebleed heights by attempting to translate *Moby-Dick* into emojis. True to the platform age, Benenson did not do the translation work himself, but crowd-sourced it on Amazon Mechanical Turk, where he had thousands of volunteers each translate a little bit of the text. The finished work—*Emoji Dick*—can be purchased for $200 in hardcover or $5 as a PDF. Meanwhile, Benenson hopes to build an emoji translation engine that will allow all literature to be turned into digi-glyphs.

Emojis may soon feel antiquated, though. GIFs—those scraps of looping video, usually stolen from films and TV shows—are no longer resigned to desktop computer use or blogging efforts like Tumblr; rapid advances in mobile tech have allowed them to be incorporated into messaging systems. On platforms like Facebook, or simply in a phone's text-message feed, users can now place a GIF as easily as they might place a smiley face. Why tap out my particular thoughts on a subject when I could simply search a library of GIFs on Giphy.com and paste a loop of Parker Posey rolling her eyes or a ripped Channing Tatum emerging from a swimming pool?

For many digital natives, messaging a friend no longer requires alphabet-based text at all. Like the emoji and the emoticon before it, the GIF is a ready-made expression, a visual cliché that saves us from the hassle of developing a personal style. Thus, Hitchcock's idea of style as "self-plagiarism" is ignored and straight-up plagiarism is practised instead. As linguistics professor Naomi Baron put it, "A GIF packages your message for you, so you don't have to figure out how to express yourself."[69] In this way the solitude of style becomes crowded by corporate properties. We give up on the possibly unique phrasing we were grasping at and become a conduit, instead, for the shared stylistic offerings of mass entertainment.

Our screen technologies are machines for connection more than independence, but they always *feel* like they're giving us both. Twitter, for example, feels like a way to broadcast my personal voice ("Hey, *world,* did you know . . ."), but it demands that I funnel that voice into a highly circumscribed format, shape, and number of characters.

In August of 2014, Twitter added an "analytics" function to their dashboard, allowing users to track in minute detail the responses elicited by their tweets. This function immediately altered my own use of the platform, bending my writing style to the pleasure of the crowd, as dictated by my analytics reports. Now that the crowd's sentiments were so evident, I sought to alter my style in ways that never would have occurred to me before. A tweet about my writing life, for instance (embossed with the hashtag #amwriting), won lots of attention, and the next day I found myself thinking: *Perhaps I should tweet a picture of my writing desk; it looks so romantic and dishevelled with that earthenware coffee mug and jam jar of wildflowers.* In this way, we become entangled in a matrix of subtle yet persuasive popularity contests; being a real out-sider—someone with a unique (or even perverse) voice—requires greater effort.

There have always been forces nudging us toward con-formity, of course; the difference is just how massively effec-tive and granular the process has become. The difference is that we now have the capacity to scrub every utterance clean of unique voice. When the system *shows* you so directly what will win the attention (and affection) of others, it takes a Herculean effort to deny it and, in Crispian terms, walk down the street in the "wrong" clothes.

Back in 1982, Neil Postman described another part of this problem when he argued that electric speed "eliminated per-sonal style, indeed, human personality itself, as an aspect of communication."[70] Like others, Postman was concerned that individual voices were abolished when communication was repackaged as data and the stories we shared were increasingly streamed along wires.

Wires like the one Samuel Morse began stringing up in 1843. Using a $30,000 grant from the U.S. government, Morse was able to erect a forty-mile-long line between Washington and Baltimore that was capable of transmitting dots and dashes in "Morse" code. His line's first news message, the result of the Whig Party convention in Baltimore, was shuttled to Washington, D.C., on May 1, 1844. The electronic news that Senator Henry Clay would be the party's presidential nominee arrived more than an hour before a steam train carrying the same report. It was a watershed moment. Morse's machine belonged to a future where communication required fewer human bodies and greater technological manipulation of the message itself. It was, quite literally, a breathtaking moment—a diminishment of the human voice.* Even via such wires, traces of our humanity did remain: Tom Standage, the digital editor at the *Economist*, has noted that individual wire operators could recognize the tapping of their counterparts in other cities by the barely discernible "signature" of their beeps.[71] Cold comfort.

New examples of this problem—the dulling of individual style as we lean toward more powerful broadcasting—are everywhere. And platform-based communication goes one step further: it doesn't just eliminate personal style, it replaces it with collaborative style. During the 2014 TED conference in Vancouver, I stood beneath a fine example: an enormous

---

* The original telegraphy ("distance writing") was achieved by the semaphore system in Napoleonic France. This was a series of towers built at high elevations that were each topped with three hinged wooden blades; these blades could be rearranged into ninety-eight different positions—plenty for a complete sign language. Superintendents at the next tower in the line could read the message with a telescope and then reproduce it at their own tower, thus passing news to the next station, and so on. Messages could quickly be sent from one end of France to the other by this means, vastly increasing the efficiency and potency of Napoleon's army. It was a half century before the system was outmoded by the electronic telegraph.

crowd-controlled light sculpture by the artist Janet Echelman
called "Skies Painted with Unnumbered Sparks." Echelman
strung a net of braided fibres—1.75 tons' worth—high above
the plaza outside the city's downtown convention centre; at
night this net pulsated with projections of moving colours,
which shifted and changed hue according to input from the
thousands of cellphones tapping beneath it. This was bolstered
by a set of speakers that also responded to cellphone activity,
emitting whale-like moans. The work, which, as the artist
noted, could "only be completed by audiences," provided a
powerful and unsettling experience—a little like peering into
a part of the light spectrum our eyes aren't built to register.
"I hope," said Echelman, "that visitors feel more connected
to those around them—to neighbours and strangers."[72] It's a
noble concept, and certainly a valid artistic expression. But
can we say the work possesses style? Is it not, rather, a kind of
anti-style? And what happens to the broader culture as massive, collaborative design becomes more common? At a website called StyleFactory, for example, users voted on which
furniture designs should be built. That collaborative, decen-
tralized approach to expression—so laudable in many ways—
shows its ugly side there: we fully express only what has been
gilded by the approval of many others.

Meanwhile, researchers at Google have created
DeepDream, which makes (pricey) art by toying with Google's
image recognition software: DeepDream looks for familiar
patterns in any image it's fed and then amps up those patterns,
producing what some have called "artificial intelligence on

LSD."[73] If you show DeepDream a beach, it may find a pattern like a dinosaur in the sand's whorls and spin that dinosaur up so it becomes more obvious. But all its "original" artwork is ultimately a bit of algorithmic playfulness, a processing of enormous reams of crowd-sourced data.

In the summer of 2015, a year after I stood beneath that web of Technicolor light during the TED conference, the artist and author Douglas Coupland handed me a book called *Search*, which he'd produced during a stint as artist-in-residence at the Google Cultural Institute's Lab, in Paris. On its double-height pages were printed enormous lists of Google searches. Coupland had selected one thousand common words and used the genius algorithms at Google to comb through billions upon billions of everyday searches to find how those words were used in the English-speaking world's Googling during one month. The most common search queries incorporating each word were neatly ranked on each page, so a page headed with the word "Answer," for instance, begins with the search query "What is the answer to life the universe and everything" and ends with "How to answer tell me about yourself question." The top query using the word "overload"? *Cute overload.* Using "should"? *How much should I weigh?* Using "child"? *Child support.* And so on.

Many billions of quiet, private questions, tabulated and ranked. It was Caitlyn Jenner and surveillance cameras and Valentine's Day and toxic shock syndrome and breakup advice and football and *Hunger Games* and Mars and global warming. The book is less a piece of writing and more history's biggest piece of found art. The experience of flipping through its pages was oddly moving—here was an expression of the hive mind buzzing to itself. The Internet had painted a self-portrait.

In the twenty-first century, does it still feel meaningful to create things from individual perspectives? Here's a thought experiment: if I took a book like Coupland's *Search* and cross-referenced it with my personal search history, I could give myself a zeitgeist ranking that would tell me how closely my curiosity mirrors the curiosity of the English-speaking world. Surely some kid in Palo Alto could string such an app together on her lunch break. . . .

What becomes interesting is our ability to sync up, to rate our own choices and beliefs against the massive collective. The more collected we become, the more solitary style feels like a pretense. Meanwhile, marketers persistently assure us that the *next* technology will promote our personal style again, that the *next* technology will allow us to become truly independent thinkers.

In 1984, Ridley Scott directed a Super Bowl commercial that promised such independence. It's a masterpiece. In a blue-grey haze, rows and rows of shaved-head automatons sit in dazed silence while Big Brother rumbles his instructions from an enormous television screen. Won't someone save these imprisoned souls? Yes! A sexy young woman (played by athlete/model Anya Major) bursts onto the scene, running toward the camera toting a sledgehammer. She hurls the thing at Big

Brother, shattering the hive mind and replacing it with . . . Apple. The then-sprightly company had positioned itself as the world's only hope against the megalithic IBM.

The commercial, called "1984" after Orwell's dystopian novel, is a marvellous example of the duplicity that tech companies deal in. From iPads to Apple Watches to the glowing logos that beam from laptops at instant-office cafés, few companies have done more to homogenize personal style than Apple. Its products determine the way we write to each other, the way we chat, the way we share news, compose music, and picture our own lives. Yet the consumption of its products is always framed with that rebellious slogan: "Think Different." Doris Lessing describes the paradox this way:

> People living in the West . . . will all emerge with an idea about themselves that goes something like this. . . . My mind is my own, my opinions are chosen by me, I am free to do as I will. . . . People in the West therefore may go through their entire lives never thinking to analyze this very flattering picture, and as a result are helpless against all kinds of pressures on them to conform in many kinds of ways.[74]

The sledgehammer does not destroy the screen: it causes it to multiply. Style in the true, Crispian sense requires that we remove ourselves from that glittering theatre altogether—or at least roll our eyes at the lame production. Switching our allegiance from one Big Brother to the next cannot purchase independent thought. Yet we have inscribed in our egos a belief that we're free and independent thinkers. And, as Lessing foresaw, this belief blinds us to the forces that would harness our every expression and gesture for their own gains.

Crisp was acquainted with the evil of "mass style," and not only in the form of violent London gangs. He came of age in a world where mass media was just gaining its mass. He saw the tech-savvy Nazis use radio to indoctrinate crowds with the party's hate. (Indeed, Hitler's minister of armaments and war production, Albert Speer, admitted at the Nuremberg Trials, "Through technical devices like the radio and loud-speaker, eighty million people were deprived of independent thought. It was thereby possible to subject them to the will of one man.")[75] And Crisp saw mass media being seized upon in the United States, too, to sell products, if not politics. Either way, he felt that mass media needed to be kept at arm's length if he was to maintain an idea of who he was as an individual. Style, after all, is not just a way of expressing oneself; it's also a way of *knowing* oneself. It is the ultimate and only rejoinder to the lynch mob's question: *Who do you think you are?*

I first fell for Quentin Crisp when I was a closeted teenager— a school librarian had included one of his memoirs in a show-case of autobiographies. In retrospect, borrowing the book did not do much for the "closet" effort. But I did not know then how easily others were able to label me—because it hadn't occurred to me that I needed a label at all. So I was free to sing along to musicals while lying on my bedroom floor (father frowning in the hallway); I was free to lisp in grade nine English that oceans were "soft sort of womb metaphors" (sniggering boys behind me); I was free to read Quentin Crisp in the hallway at lunch. Because I enjoyed the special obliviousness of the solitary.

I was nothing like Crisp, of course. Crisp was audacious, rude, forthright; I was a pimply boy in oversized West Beach hoodies. Still, he was the first to convince me that being an awkward outsider could be valuable—even remarkable. I would stare at the photo of Crisp on the paperback's cover— that permissive face all done up in rouge. It was a kind of incantation. A calling up of some needful otherness.

Only now that I look back at Crisp's life do I realize he's much more than a message in a bottle for gay youths. He ought to be a patron saint for modern times. We could all stand to care a little less about what the hectoring crowds think.

As for me, I've stopped checking my Twitter analytics, for a start; the "follower" counter ticks slowly backward sometimes, a banal admonishment. The Twitter-shift was such a tiny thing, but even that has been enough to return some portion of myself, bringing more of the raw "I" back. And the less I looked to the reactions of others, the more I interrogated the modes of expression that I had thought were "natural" to me. My online posts weren't my "voice" at all; they were learned responses to the positive feedback of others. I wanted to dodge that now; I wanted to become my own algorithm.

Crisp pitied those who couldn't carve out solitary moments for themselves; he saw *them* as victims, not himself. When he watched his hyper-connected friends flicking on the radio or using the television as background company, he saw that the point of these devices was "not to entertain but to drown the ticking of all clocks."[76] He found that most of the people he met were distressed by empty time—so-called "spare" time. Terrified of that blank space, they went to the movies. In a 1983 interview, he complained of Americans: "They will sit in front of a television and say 'Isn't it awful' and still they don't take their eyes from it."[77] (Later in the interview he notes that such people are only lonely because they don't know how to be alone.) It's through this transfixion that members of the public bathe themselves in the zeitgeist and ignore the solitary workshop where they might forge an independent style.

Of course, none of this can be managed without feeling impolite at first—maybe even offensive. But to achieve independence like Quentin Crisp did, we must shrug off that desire to please—to be liked or shared or followed. It can be terrifying to be so disruptive, though perhaps not so terrifying as the alternative.

6

You Have to Taste This

John McCarthy, the American computer scientist who coined the term *artificial intelligence*, had the gall to insist that pieces of technology could hold opinions and beliefs. This was 1979, and he was one of the middle-aged wizards of the computer boom; at the time many exaggerated claims were bouncing down the halls of MIT and Stanford (McCarthy taught at both). In a paper, he wrote: "Machines as simple as thermostats can be said to have beliefs."[78]

John Searle, the American philosopher, was less of an optimist and found the notion hard to swallow. One day he asked McCarthy to be precise: "What beliefs does your thermostat have?" And he was surprised by the ready answer: "My thermostat has three beliefs," said McCarthy. "It's too hot in here, it's too cold in here, and it's just right in here."[79]

Can a piece of technology have a preference for one thing or another? The distinction between human and computer intentions is growing hazy. That much was obvious when my friend showed off his new Nest thermostat, which was patched into Google's cloud and had been tracking his whereabouts in order to optimize his house's energy consumption. "Nest doesn't like it when I come home early," said my friend, tapping at the glowing black puck on his living room wall. "It really likes me to have a pattern. That way it can make better decisions."

This tiny slip—*it can make better decisions*—is crucial, because if we begin by allowing a thermostat to have a belief, we start to allow more complex technologies to have more complex beliefs, and just as my friend feels swayed to regulate his patterns because a trumped-up thermostat has a certain preference, we can find ourselves swayed in all sorts of places where we once made more personal choices.

Nowhere is this creepier than the arena of *taste*. If we think that a computer program—so much more rational, so much better informed—*believes* one thing to be better than another, then the choices we make online about what books to read, what songs to listen to, what movies to watch become less independent and more manipulated. Suggestions on Netflix and iTunes and Amazon—all crowd-sourced and data-crunched—start to feel natural and neutral. If you believe a piece of technology can have a belief, then it's only a tiny step before you start to believe its belief is more important than your own. We've all acquiesced at some point to the "you'd like this" suggestion of an algorithm.

So. Why do we like to invest our technologies with beliefs in the first place? To try to understand, I went to John Searle (the detractor in that old thermostat debate). I wanted to know if, four decades later, his position had changed. After all, we aren't just talking about thermostats anymore: artificial intelligence programs now tackle scientific mysteries; they write novels; they paint portraits; they even mark undergrad essays. Could they now be said to have beliefs after all?

"No, I still think those views are idiotic."

The eighty-three-year-old Professor Searle is clean-shaven and straight talking. He sits in his Moses Hall offices on the humming Berkeley campus and adjusts his tone minutely: "There was never any animosity between McCarthy and me."

I frown slightly and ask, "But you don't believe a machine could one day think?"

"Ah, that's the wrong question. Of *course* a machine can think. *We* are machines, and *we* think. The question is, can a *computer* think? And absolutely no, it cannot."

"So what's the important difference? What's so limiting about a computer?"

"Computers are processing computations. They are shuffling symbols in a circuit. You can't get to consciousness by shuffling symbols. For consciousness, and *beliefs*, you need a causal mechanism."

"How do you know our sense of self comes from a causal mechanism and not just a bunch of data bouncing around in our brains?"

"It's very simple. I can mess with the causes and it messes up the effects. Each day I drink some cabernet sauvignon and I see how it messes with my consciousness. Our brains are machines like the wings of a bird or the pumping heart in your chest. We won't be able to build an artificial intelligence until we know precisely the mechanics of our brain. But people don't understand that. They think they can get there through abstract numbers. But you need the bioengineering, the chemistry."

Searle believes that the Turing test—Alan Turing's famous thought experiment designed to prove whether a given computer has achieved "intelligence" or not—is "a massive error." In a Turing test, an anonymous human is hidden behind a curtain, along with a computer. Another human then has a conversation with them both via text message. If this person can't tell which respondent is the human, then the computer has passed the test and is deemed "intelligent." But to Searle, such a test misses the point: it supposes that, given enough processing power, our computers can one day hold genuine beliefs of their own. But big data does not impress the philosopher.

The fallacy of "thinking computers" could be a dangerous one. The more we believe that our computers and online platforms have beliefs of their own, the more likely we are to bend our own solitary taste and preferences to the seductive, mysterious offerings we receive through glowing screens. And, because these technologies have arrived at their supposed "preferences" by crowd-sourcing, by the sorting of massive data dumps, the result must be that independent, solitary taste is dwarfed by collective taste.

Pine or teak? Polyester or silk? Carrie Underwood or Antonio Vivaldi? By such superficial choices do we formulate our ideas of each other—and of ourselves. Recently, moored on the sofa, Kenny and I came to the agreement that we could not abide any further episodes of *Chopped*. We started scanning iTunes for a movie and this happened: One of us would say, "What about the armadillo doc? You *love* armadillos." Then the other would shoot the idea down by citing its aggregated rating. "*Two* stars? We need *some* standards." I can't call it a debate. It was merely navigation; it didn't involve our opinions, our critique of the trailer, our knowledge of the director—it was just the repetition of a highly prescriptive rating system. At the same time, we were picking through containers of Thai food from a restaurant that had been selected from the top of a Yelp list and we were loosely listening to a playlist sponsored by the curatorial geniuses behind the Mr. Clean products. Nothing we were consuming appeared to be directly related to our personal taste—rather, we were gumming some kind of sanctioned cultural porridge. The question was: who cooked it?

Was it my choice when we finally settled on *Pitch Perfect 2*? Was it the collective decision of some swarming crowd? Or, stranger yet, was the decision made by an algorithm's own alien aesthetics?

I spoke with Matt Atchity, who is the editor-in-chief at the film review aggregator Rotten Tomatoes. It's his job to be (in his words) "a town crier," helping the world to learn what masses of film critics from across the land have, en masse, decided about *Mad Max* or *Avatar 2*. He does media appearances and folk ask him for his own opinions—but he and his website mainly serve as a filter through which the opinions of hundreds of professional reviewers can become a single average. The solitary taste of particular critics is rounded out by the flow of mass opinion, like so many jagged pebbles polished under the river. "I feel I'm a herald," Atchity told me. "I don't consider myself a critic, but I fulfill that function for a number of outlets." And for millions of visitors to his site. And also for millions more (like Kenny and me) who choose films based on the Rotten Tomatoes ratings that have been imported to Netflix and tagged onto the description of every film. A recent Nielsen report, surveying twenty-eight thousand people in fifty-six countries, found that such online reviews are second only to personal recommendations when it comes to trusted brand information.[80] This trust had increased 15 per cent since the previous such survey, four years earlier.

When we allow sites like Rotten Tomatoes to decide which movies, dinners, and songs we consume, we go along with the myth that our decisions are being made by neutral and unbiased guides. Perhaps we think this is a cure for elitism—a flattening of the critical landscape. It's rational, it's the crowd, and so it's undeniably *what is best*. We find ourselves nudged toward the quantifiable. Our aggregators of taste have allowed for this myth to grow so strong, in fact, that it becomes invisible: a myth of natural, inarguable taste, doled out in star ratings and unimpeachable bestseller rankings.

But we forget: taste is never natural. If we aren't making aesthetic decisions for ourselves, then someone or something else is doing it for us. Bestseller lists have guided readers since the nineteenth century, and mass media has influenced everything from pet food selection to travel destinations, at least since the invention of newspapers. But a new and more pernicious level of taste management now prevails. The world leans across the table, holds a spoon an inch from your closed lips, and gives you a determined smile: *You have to taste this.*

Why do we open our mouths?

Out of necessity. There's such a deluge of cultural content, we cannot parse it on our own. In the 1980s, researchers began talking about the "information-load paradigm," which refers to the saturation limit after which people can't absorb more information.[81] This was a new conceit in the eighties—a response to the maelstrom of material suddenly being produced. Today we can likewise talk about our "culture-load." There are only so many songs, books, movies, memes we can take in and form opinions on before the culture-load buries us under a mountain of must-reads and essential videos.

Thus squashed, we encounter what psychologist Barry Schwartz calls the paradox of choice. We thought that more options would produce more freedom, and thus more happiness (215 soda options = American Dream). But the reality of such splendorous choice is quite different. In fact, according to Schwartz, the flood of choices that a screen age citizen faces "produces paralysis rather than liberation."[82] Consider, for example, the art and music and literature being shared online in the one minute it takes you to read this paragraph: 72 hours of YouTube video will be uploaded; 5.5 million Snapchat videos will be viewed; and 216,000 photos will go up on Instagram.[83] Simply glance at the streaming content of a single minute, all of which you missed while you were focused on these sentences, and your gut tightens—you've already fallen grievously behind. You cast about for something—*anything*—to make sense of all these scraps of art and heritage and supposed beauty. But the Tower of Babel has become a City of Babel. We race desperately from door to door.

One company that stepped in as a guide to Babel City was Songza, the music-streaming site that was bought by Google and incorporated into their Play Music platform in 2015. Songza produced hundreds of playlists that users select not based on interest in particular bands or composers but based on their current feelings or activities. *Cleaning the house? This'll help.* It's an addictive and intuitive approach; it made Songza a friendly curator to the masses. You don't need to know which bands are cool, you just need to know you're picking music for "cocktails with cool people."

Co-founder Elias Roman hardly looks like a tech geek (he's muscled and handsome), and his conversation is equally surprising. He told me that "the oppression of choice" is what he thinks about most when he goes to work. It's a phrase that echoes—but darkens—Schwartz's "paradox of choice." Whereas Schwartz (who's about twice Roman's age, at seventy) predicts a world where crowds of options lead to disaffection, Roman sees that our culture-load is such a problem that it becomes a kind of maltreatment, something that can numb the senses, make us less alive. Songza's curatorial approach—those activity-based or mood-based song lists—were a way to cut through the oceans of material, make your choices for you. "Songza needs to know you better than you know yourself," Roman explained.

Mostly, I've been happy to let wayfinding systems like his guide me through Babel City. What book should I read? Easy: Amazon purchasing patterns have (for the moment) led to the promotion of *Harry Potter and the Cursed Child*. And which songs would make the best soundtrack for my run? Nothing simpler: I type "running playlist" into the YouTube app and click one that half a million others found useful. But the more I think about the aggregating forces in my life, the more I wonder how they shape my ideas about what is *worthwhile* and what *should be ignored*. Where is my own taste? And just how easy is it for a crowd to change a person's mind?

In 1951, fifty male students at Harvard University were taken, one by one, into a little room and subjected to what they believed to be a vision test. Each student was joined by six actors who were supposedly taking the test, too. Professor Solomon Asch, a Guggenheim fellow and social psychology pioneer, had prepped these actors, instructing them on how they should answer each question in advance. And so the test began: Here is a line on a piece of paper. Here are three lines on this other piece of paper, each line a different length. Now, can you tell us, sir, which of these three lines is the same length as the line you see on the first piece of paper? The answer was incredibly straightforward; there was no visual trickery at play. All participants were able to see which lines were matches. But then Asch's experiment really began: the actors began making patently false claims; eventually the majority claimed that the answer was clearly line C when anyone with working eyes could tell the answer was line B. A full three-quarters of participants changed their minds at least once in order to conform to the incorrect crowd.[84] Meanwhile, in a control group where the actors gave no wrong answers, less than 1 per cent of participants made a mistake. Subsequent studies back up Asch's startling findings. Our opinions are so easily bent by the certitude of public pressure.

If it's that simple to convince a person that a short line is a long line, what chance do I have when the crowd tells me colouring books for adults are now a thing? New arbiters of taste are constantly emerging online, offering comforting ways to brave the content floods, all the while nudging aside more solitary, aesthetic decisions. *This line is longer, isn't it?* murmurs the crowd. And we nod our silent assent.

Sometimes these nudges come from a select group of thinking humans, as with Songza's curated playlists, but other times the nudges appear to come from ourselves: we may find ourselves inside a "filter bubble." These mysterious entities (first discussed by Eli Pariser, the chief executive of the news site Upworthy) are composed of the many invisible "personalized" algorithms that curate your view of things online, filtering the content you consume in order to optimize the chance you'll be shown things you're likely to click on. If the algorithm knows you'll click on an episode of *Girls* or the new Anne Rice novel, then that's what you're going to see. All this feels "personal" because you keep on seeing things that you want to consume—*ooh, more of those Willy Wonka GIFs I like!*—but at the same time you become trapped inside an algorithmically defined notion of your own taste. Put in a less wonky way: you won't be exposed to things you *don't know*, things you *haven't loved yet*. Personal growth becomes stunted, and the idea of what you "like" is grotesquely caricatured.

In the end, the crowding of content in the age of screens can be navigated only by impersonal measures—by aggregating and subjugating our personal taste into a lump of crowd-taste. We turn "what I like" into "what we like"—or, worse, "what *one* likes." We can hack our way through a world's worth of content only with the aid of the very online technologies that produced the flood in the first place. Inevitably, that giving over of our independence nudges us away from personal taste decisions and toward adherence to the group. We receive our decisions through our screens and then accept them as our own.

This is how a new myth about taste emerges—a myth that the online world can pulp up billions of human choices and deliver a single, *natural* taste. (*Donnie Darko* is the third-best coming-of-age film—result of 2,579 votes; the new Tommy Hilfiger men's wallet deserves 4.3 stars out of 5—result of 2,377 votes.) Who would deny such data-driven pronouncements? In this way, our phones, our tablets, our platform technologies become oracles of taste.

Twenty years down the road, the mechanics of this oracular taste will fade from notice, becoming an unacknowledged mythology: these just *are* the things we prefer. Ever primed to believe in our own independence, our own big faultless ability to choose for ourselves what is best, we'll believe that our choices are our own. We'll become numb to the winds that sway us.

Maybe this is a good place to ask, who cares?

If our notions have always been bullied this way or that by outside forces, so what if our technologies start subtly shaping our ideas about good and bad TV shows, books, and fabric swatches? Maybe we *want* their ideas. (Who has better ideas about temperature than a thermostat?) Well, consider this warning from Neil Postman:

> A young man who believes Madonna to have reached the highest pinnacle of musical expression lacks the sensibility to distinguish between the ascent and descent of humanity. . . . Our youth must be shown that not all worthwhile things are instantly accessible and that there are levels of sensibility unknown to them.[85]

Putting aside Postman's grouchy attitude toward Madonna, he does make an important point. Some "levels of sensibility" cannot be shared and liked online, or turned into a funny GIF. Not all things that are worth loving are easy to love right away. It's only a small portion of the larger culture that can

108

thrive on platform technologies. Meanwhile, those things that cannot be reduced to 140 characters—the spinning chaos we sense standing before a Jackson Pollock canvas, the harrowing perfection we glimpse when reading a Virginia Woolf novel— can be loved only once we've *earned* them. Online, we blow in a wind of mass culture that is so pleasant and dreamlike— with mass taste projecting only the easy-to-consume—that we have little time for those more difficult, solitary tastes. Matthew Crawford notes in his book *The World Beyond Your Head* that the process of acquiring adult taste is in fact the opposite of entertainment—it requires work and education. "Does it have a future?" he asks. "The advent of engineered, hyperpalatable mental stimuli compels us to ask the question."[86] It also compels us to ask what we miss out on when we ditch Crawford's idea of educated taste in favour of a taste based on mass entertainment and mass judgment.

The title of James Surowiecki's book *The Wisdom of Crowds* often gets turned into a sound bite, suggesting that the masses know best. But those who have read more than the back cover know that Surowiecki is subtler than that. He describes how "groups that are too much alike find it harder to keep learning, because each member is bringing less and less new information to the table. Homogeneous groups . . . become progressively less able to investigate alternatives."[87] As we allow our personal taste to be dictated by online crowds, we'd be wise to keep that progression in mind. What began in the twentieth century with companies like McDonald's and Disney producing massively shared food and entertainment has been followed in the twenty-first century with companies like Google and Amazon producing massively shared taste.

The difference between Before and After is that today we need to safeguard our inner weirdo, seal it off and protect it from being buffeted. Learn an old torch song that nobody knows; read a musty, out-of-print detective novel; photograph a honey-perfect sunset and show it to no one. We may need to build new and stronger weirdo cocoons, in which to entertain our private selves. Beyond the sharing, the commenting, the constant thumbs-upping, beyond all that distracting gilt, there are stranger things waiting to be loved.

7

Stranger in a Strange Land

Mapping

Midway through Lewis Carroll's absurdist novel *Sylvie and Bruno*, the book's narrator meets an odd fellow called Mein Herr, who hails from another planet but has a keen interest in ours. The pair ends up discussing the human art of map-making:

> "That's another thing we've learned from *your* Nation," said Mein Herr, "map-making. But we've carried it much further than *you*. What do you consider the *largest* map that would be really useful?"
>
> "About six inches to the mile."
>
> "Only *six inches*!" exclaimed Mein Herr. "We very soon got to six *yards* to the mile. Then we tried a *hundred* yards to the mile. And then came the grandest idea of all! We actually made a map of the country, on the scale of *a mile to the mile*!"

"Have you used it much?" I enquired.

"It has never been spread out, yet," said Mein Herr: "the farmers objected: they said it would cover the whole country, and shut out the sunlight!"[88]

When I first read this scene I felt there was something very familiar about the map Mein Herr describes. For weeks it bothered me. And then one day, while trying to find a Starbucks (read: toilet) in a dodgy suburban neighbourhood, I saw that Mein Herr was describing the Google Maps app on my phone.

Making the connection took me so long because, to look at them, the mapping systems we adopt today don't *seem* country-sized at all. In fact, they're some of the smallest physical maps we've ever employed—only a few square inches of glowing glass. We might also look past our handheld devices to Google's stadium-sized data centres, which house the dozens of petabytes of street photos and satellite images that allow their map to function—20 petabytes in 2012, when the number was last released. (To imagine the size of a single petabyte, picture the entire contents of the Library of Congress, and then quadruple it.) Although we aren't aware of them when we glance at our phones, these petabytes truly do cover everything—every cul-du-sac and alley, every corner store and vegetable garden. Each previously mysterious inch of the planet is charted and displayed, managed and labelled, by an authority far removed from our personal experience.

When a mapping system is so ubiquitous that we turn to it at the slightest hesitation, it becomes more than an aid. It becomes another enemy of solitude—for it insists that you will never be lost, you will never slip away. We have engineered a constant guide that undoes the solitary traveller's ability to be lost at all. It seems we have constructed a map very like Mein Herr's, for it threatens to smother all that it depicts.

In the winter of 2014 my work took me to a conference of publishers in London. Getting myself to the convention centre and back, and then to meetings with an editor and dinner with a friend, was all managed exclusively via Google Maps. I enjoyed a kind of magical dependence that involved following each step of the journey with an obedience I hadn't known since childhood: turn right, walk 50 yards; wait two minutes at the southbound platform of Oxford Circus; board the train at 11:52 a.m. . . . Something easy and dull had stolen over my experience, a phantom arm across the shoulder, a constant companion saying, "Allow me." There was no need to be lost or take on the blushing anxieties of earlier travel.

A post-conference weekend in Paris was the same but more so. Disembarking from the train from London, I invited a friendly app to guide me to a hotel near the Pompidou. There was nothing unusual about speaking English to the hotel attendant; indeed, it seemed impertinent to force this clearly bilingual woman, with her lacquered clockwork of hair, to pretend she needed my "Je suis ici pour le check-in."

The next morning, Yelp guided me toward a charming café in the Marais. There, wizard-like, I held my phone over the menu and waited for Google Translate to melt the words into English. When the waiter arrived, I spoke into my phone and had it repeat my words to the grinning *garçon* in a soft, robotic French. Later, at the Louvre, I allowed a Nintendo-sponsored guidance system to track my steps up the centuries-old Daru staircase as I squinted confusedly at its glowing blue you-are-here dot. I stared a minute at an image of the Winged Victory of Samothrace, whose velvety marble bust had been made minutely jagged on the pixelated screen, before realizing the real thing was hovering in front of me. I had, in sum, zero mastery over the city or its culture but could be shepherded into a sense of ease that would have been unthinkable even five years earlier.

And yet only on my (guided) journey back to Heathrow Airport did it strike me that I'd not always behaved this way, that travel had once meant something entirely different.

It was the fruit cart that did it. Walking down a London sidewalk, I passed a pyramid of apples and, with Proustian force, the memory of an earlier journey to that city unfolded around me. I froze and pocketed the phone, looked around with a slack jaw. Suddenly, I knew this street. I had been here before.

I was twenty the first time, lost and alone. I had slept briefly in a rank Earls Court hostel, having arrived from Canada the night before. The top of my left ear stung with a new piercing, and an enormous pack wagged oppressively on my shoulders as I hunted for the bus stop where my journey to the Lake District was meant to begin. The stop had slipped, somehow, several blocks away from where it was meant to be, and I'd been jogging in a slight fury of confusion. I missed the bus I was meant for. But a man at an apple stand (complete with Cockney accent) pointed me down a crooked lane toward my goal. On the second bus I met a boy called Jonathan and fell promptly in love: by Stonehenge we had abandoned the tour. For the next several weeks, as our affair played out, we seemed to be always lost.

We were lost the first time we kissed, in a field of hip-high grass miles from some pub-attic hostel; we lost ourselves on sheep-freckled hills and in the gardens of *Brideshead*-worthy estates; we lost ourselves in the midnight streets of Edinburgh while Elton John sang "Crocodile Rock" beyond the stone walls of the city's castle. We were always lost and that was somehow intrinsic to our affection for each other. Certainly I was lost, again, when Jonathan chose his Catholic faith over me and disappeared. There was no Facebook or Instagram with which to stalk him. Instead, I slumped along the bank of the Thames in my oversized sweaters and injured looks, listening to a tape of sorrowful Jeff Buckley songs that Jonathan had given me the night he flew home to Australia. I was lost and in love and torturously alone.

That was when being lost changed from a young person's thrill to an existential thing—I was heartbroken and wanted desperately to be found.

Sometimes we are, by a brief miracle, young and in love—and so gravitate toward the thrill of being lost. But most of our lives are ruled by the desire to *not* be lost—to be made secure within a bewildering city, or in the awkward pangs of middle age.

The desire is as old as us. Paleolithic people in Lascaux, France, mapped the stars they saw each night by painting dots on the walls of caves. We've been at it ever since. And every map, whatever its veracity, is a straining to reduce enormous and uncertain surroundings into something legible. But when we create an abstract representation of something that's too big for us to navigate on our own (a map of London streets, a chart of the heavens), we should admit that, as Marshall McLuhan put it, these tools have "the power to numb human awareness."[89] (The numbness may be what we're looking for.) We see more—but only through a waxy lens. We are safe and held, but also impoverished.

Today, that desire to be un-lost, to be tagged in the wilderness of our lives, has been sated in the most gratifying way yet. If you like, all the wonders of the world can be labelled and displayed for you in bright heaps of pixels. And travel, meanwhile, becomes an exercise in *not* being lost; we become confident, adoring the permanent tracking of parental, cloud-based systems. It's an addictive and supremely comforting feeling. But when I froze at that fruit stand and was flooded with memories of a previous, untethered time, I was forced again to wonder: what do we hand over in the bargain? What changed between my lost-in-the-field trip to England and the Google Maps version? Was it just that I was older, less open, now? Or had something larger than myself changed in the intervening years?

In her University of Oregon office, Professor Amy Lobben sits before an enormous, out-of-date chalkboard. She watches the new crop of students navigate a latticework of paths on the lawn outside her window. A floor-to-ceiling shelf is filled with books, old cartographic instruments, and antique maps.

We are discussing the ways that humans form an understanding of their surroundings. Lobben quickly gets to the point: "Your private mental map is never going to look like a Google Map. The brain just does not encode space that way." She describes, instead, mental maps that are skewed by whatever is meaningful to the individual. "It's a very visceral, fundamental human thing," in which places that are important are emphasized and distances between home and work may be shrunk by the experience of rapid transit. "If you go out into the world with your senses open," she says, "you're going to encode a mental map that's made with whatever types of info your brain likes to attend to, and your map will be different from those of other people." Your mind is constantly retouching its personal map—it maintains a living, morphing atlas that only you can read.

The maps that Google now works on attempt a "personalization," too. They're modelled after our individual click behaviour, with each map's contents slightly altered to show us things we seem to prefer. Preferential treatment is also given, however, to the shops and places that folk in your social network like. In the fall of 2015, a couple of years after the initial announcement about personalized maps, Google senior product manager Murali Viswanathan wrote about the "curated selections" Google could offer when users opened their mapping system: "Having the best local guide is great, but what's better: having the best local guide *for you*."[90] This sounds freeing. But remember: places that Google's algorithms decide aren't "your kind of thing" will now be harder to find. And as media critic Evgeny Morozov has noted, as long as advertising remains the mainstay of Google's profits, they're not likely to care whether we discover things that cannot be monetized.

"Personalization" like that can rapidly get out of hand. Professor Jerry Brotton (author of *A History of the World in 12 Maps*) feels we're going through a shift as fundamental as the fifteenth-century switch from hand-drawn maps to the printed variety: "Maps have become inhuman . . . driven by the imperatives of e-commerce rather than a confrontation with physical, terrestrial reality."[91] And so, when Google is the main distributor of maps—as opposed to governments or even a spate of competing companies—our wayfinding becomes merely an encounter with a vast string of digital shops. It's not difficult to imagine a future in which uncooperative stores or restaurants, or even landmarks, are simply deleted from view. The difference, then, between your brain's personalization and Google's is that the Google experience is really a hybrid of your brain's choices and a corporation's.

Another way of understanding this difference is to look at the perspective that maps like Google's force us to adopt. In the mapping world, that clean bird's-eye view that Google uses is called an allocentric (meaning "outside the self") perspective. The perspective that humans have when they walk down a street is called egocentric. When a fumbling tourist unfolds a paper map, he is actually using a symbiosis of the two perspectives. He looks up, looks down, looks up, thinking, "Oh crap, I'm lost" or "Ha! Aren't I clever." A richer understanding of place evolves from the fusing of the two vantages.

But Google Maps, argues Professor Lobben, has created an entirely new, and far more limited, experience of navigation. "In one sense it does help people to simply press the Easy button," she says. "But I think that Google Maps is very hindering, too. You get from one location to another and to do that you press Go. And for the next twenty minutes you are following instructions, head down almost the whole way. I work with map dorks all day and we've all seen this, it's something most people do now. We've turned into navigation zombies. Without thinking, you follow what Google Maps tells you to do."*

"Navigation zombie" doesn't *sound* good. But I ask Lobben what the concrete problems are with obeying Google's instructions.

---

* Lobben is no Luddite, though: she is working on an app that produces personalized routes for people with disabilities. She considers it "almost shameful" that such an app—filtering out or highlighting things that hinder accessibility to an environment—has not been developed.

It impacts us in two ways, she tells me. The first, and most obvious, is that it's cold—the user soars up to enjoy an attractively allocentric vision, giving up on the egocentric viewpoint that would expose us to the laughter of that dog walker or the way neighbourhood children invent games on the sidewalk. But the second problem (which is harder to notice) is that, while it makes us feel like navigational gods, Google Maps actually allows our wayfinding skills to atrophy. "And wayfinding" says Lobben, "is inherently human. It is so important to everyday existence and is probably key to human evolution. Our ancestors' ability to get to a food source and back, for example, would have been essential. But then you insert a tool that allows you to wayfind without thinking and you're no longer improving that skill." If successfully navigating a mysterious landscape has always been an inherent part of our survival—if it has, in fact, allowed our ancestors to survive and pass on their genes—then to give up on that skill is to give up on a part of our selves.

Our conversation turns briefly to the antique maps that Lobben has on display. I comment on the sea monsters and giants that old mapmakers drew in areas they were fuzzy about—visual metaphors for their own anxieties and ignorance. I ask, "Where are the sea monsters in a Google map, do you think?"

"There don't seem to be any," she says. "It seems to all be there. But that's the monster itself, isn't it? The map speaks with such authority. There is a whole generation that's grown up with Google without even being aware of it. They just allow Google to show them what the world looks like. Whereas previous generations grew up with many different maps that all looked different so we knew these were only *ideas* of how the world could be organized. Just ideas. I grew up looking at so many different kinds of maps that I knew there were different ways of looking at the world. And you had to make up your own mind. People today, certainly all my students, think there is *a* map. Well, there is not *a* map."

Long before Google Maps created a sense of shared purity in our wayfinding experience, other maps were pushing toward the One True Vision.

Consider the story of sixteenth-century cartographer Gerardus Mercator, who produced an extraordinary new map of the world in 1569. His map snapped distant shores into focus as never before. For the first time, the "rhumb lines" that sailors traced on globes to navigate the open ocean were made two-dimensional—and this allowed for enormous strides in seafaring. Many earlier maps had been practically worthless for ocean-spanning navigation, with every error and misperception potentially ending in shipwreck. The Mercator map came at just the right time, aiding sailors and, by extension, whole nations in their grasping, empire-building enterprise. There were, of course, a few fantastical decorations in its margins: we see a tiny illustration of Triton riding his horse across the South Pacific; there are fearsome sea monsters, too; dastardly cannibals in the New Indies; and giants in Patagonia

(Magellan's tall tales were to blame for those). Naturally, the farther away from Europe, the more liberal Mercator's fancy became. But there were other, more insidious ways the Mercator map—which became our most common vision of the planet—was completely inaccurate.

It wasn't until 1973 that German historian Arno Peters made it clear to the public how flattening a three-dimensional globe onto a single plane the way Mercator's map does will vastly distort the size of countries, depending on their distance from the equator. We've all grown up studying a map that makes Greenland look roughly the size of Africa; Greenland is in fact fourteen times smaller. Similarly, in a Mercator map Europe appears only slightly smaller than South America, while, in fact, South America has double Europe's land mass.

The "corrected" vision that Peters proposed, with Europe squished up into insignificance at the upper end of the map, is now widely promoted by UNESCO. The "Peters projection" has its own questionable mathematics (areas near the poles and equator still get stretched), but that's just the point: as Professor Brotton has said, "No map is any better or worse than any other map. It's just about what agenda it pursues."[92] The Mercator map, with its European countries on top and its odd diminishment of the poorer countries that were set for domination, can now be read as a creepy bit of Eurocentric thinking—a leftover from the days of empire. Just as gods and monsters enlivened its borders, the very dimensions of the world Mercator presented were warped by his particular bias.

And yet we go on denying our biases and search, instead, for a vision of the world we can call impersonal, objective, true for everyone at once.

Professor Lobben tells me her father worked for a company that constantly transplanted the family to cities in Europe, Asia, and Africa. So, from the age of eight onward, she was presented with a mosaic of cultural perspectives. Today, when confronted with the singular perspective of a dominant mapping app, she frowns: "This is all about much more than choosing what colour to paint the different countries. The people who are in a position to decide how you engage with the world, those people have a lot of power." A myth of purity has arisen, she insists, a myth that tells us: this is the world, this is how to navigate it, this is the shared approach.

But we can revolt against this sense of clarity and ease by going off by ourselves and getting lost. People go down rabbit holes, through looking-glasses, and out the back of closets all the time. Outside the strict management and positioning of algorithmic forces, our minds are permitted to craft truly idiosyncratic maps of the world. This is how we discover that which others have not mapped out for us, how we stumble upon the unknown. There can be, of course, no formula for deciphering this unknown's value, no proof. That is the great irony of arguments like Professor Lobben's or Professor Brotton's. How, after all, do you quantify the value of a lost traveller? It would be as impossible as capturing the stars on the walls of a cave. Or describing the disoriented feeling of being in love for the first time.

As for Jonathan and me—back in our English ramblings—we seemed to need that unmooring, that wandering experience, in order to step into our fuller lives. We travel, after all, to escape the uncompromising corners of our domestic origins—the rigid ordering of the households where we were raised. We seem to *need* agitation, strangeness, rough texture, in order to grow, to explore.

Wanderings are built into the most fundamental stories we tell ourselves about human growth. We all know that a hero must leave home and trek through uncharted territory to fulfill their potential. Yet the "hero's journey" that Achilles and Luke Skywalker experience is not an option for most of us. Usually our travels are only small and hopeful interruptions, tiny chance glimpses of alternate selves. Mostly, we cling to the gossamer threads dropped down by GPS satellites; we insist on being moored and accounted for. We map out our every journey. And even if there were a few wild weeks in some foreign country during our greener days, we all find ourselves retreating, exhausted, into the embrace of guidance systems in the end.

We make this retreat not only to feel safe but also to feel in control of an uncontrollable world. Sometimes, these days, I skim lazily, happily across the world's twirling surface on the marvellous Google Earth app:

- I fly over the lush foliage of the Nuuanu Reservoir in Honolulu and land among the staid minivans parked around the local high school.
- Next—zoom!—I hop over to Cape Evans in Antarctica and visit Scott's Hut, a relic of an earlier explorer's time that's been petrified in ice since 1912.
- And then—ziip!—I skid across the Syrian Desert, coming to rest by a mural of Saddam Hussein on a building just around the corner from the Abu Ghraib prison.

It is intoxicating. I feel god-like; such agency! To a person living in the relatively data-impoverished 1980s, this glory of access might represent a lifetime of travels. To me, it is the work of three minutes. I travel without leaving the comfort of my desk, without ever putting myself in the awkward position of becoming "a stranger," never mind the crushing loneliness and hardship required of real travellers. This wizardry represents what naturalist Robert Michael Pyle calls "the extinction of experience." What began as an ever-increasing digital management of my European jaunt reaches its nadir with the legless stupor of a laptop safari. And yet I'm left asking . . .

- What does it smell like at the top of the Nuuanu Reservoir?
- What does blistering cold feel like right before curtains of Antarctic snow turn your thoughts drunkenly toward mortal terror?
- And what looks would the locals give me as I stepped along the sidewalk outside Abu Ghraib?

These things are not stored in Google's data banks.

Happily, even the most omnipresent map can be tucked away from time to time. In *Sylvie and Bruno*, after the mapmakers decide to map out their country at a scale of "a mile to the mile," they realize their enormous work would smother their country. They regroup. And then they have their epiphany: "We now use the country itself, as its own map," explains Mein Herr, "and I assure you it does nearly as well."[93] Ordering and labelling and rational guides are laid aside. What remains after all that effort is the raw, chaotic, and morphing world, which can be known personably or not at all.

Like Carroll's industrious mapmakers, we try and try to fit the heaving chaos of the real world into an abstract expression that everyone can share. And yet—whether in the deserted temples of Angkor, or in Istanbul's Grand Bazaar, or simply in the backyard of a house in Detroit—personal experience always overflows. The personal experience can never be fully mapped. Only when we choose to work on our solo, mental maps, eschewing prefab, crowd-sourced options, do we open ourselves to the sheer terrible wonderful strangeness that previous generations of travellers took for granted. We inherit, then, one of the finest kinds of solitude—the thrumming challenge of the uncharted.

Self-Tracking

In our age of screens, the desire to chart things extends well beyond maps. We comment, we log, and we post in order to tell our nervous selves: I am known, I am quantifiable, I am *right here*. (Not lost. Never alone.)

An entire culture of self-tracking has emerged. From Instagrams of decorative cappuccino foam to reports on exercise routines, we wish to gild formerly solitary moments with online commentary. More than twenty-five million data-gathering Fitbit bracelets, for example, score the quality of users' sleep and can then report circadian rhythms to the world.[94] Such excesses of self-tracking are part of the larger urge toward orientation that Professor Lobben describes.

As that self-tracking culture matures, future generations may become addicted to knowing—in minute detail—where they stand. Why not know your carbon footprint from minute to minute as you fly to Shanghai? Why not have your car pick you up the moment the concert is over, or be alerted to the fact that you're standing in the same grocery store lineup your best friend stood in three weeks ago? Tracking can be magical and empowering—that which is tracked is cared for, kept company. The alternative (we imagine) is discomfort, anxiety, and abandonment. Missing objects, confusing tuk-tuk rides, countless disconnects that leave us helpless and flailing. The lost souls of the past are, by this estimation, mired in a pitiable incertitude.

Once we're able to monitor every portion of our lives, it can even feel like a kind of laziness, a negligence, to refrain. So we're compelled from infancy to join this cult of tracking. Gone is the scratchy, audio-only Fisher-Price baby monitor; HD videos stream to the smartphones of watchful parents in the living room. In 2014, devices like Mimo and MonBaby were released, too—smart infant sleepwear that uses Bluetooth to issue reports on breathing, heart rate, and movements. These devices seem to engender increased anxiety about the baby's well-being while they also abstract the monitoring process. I've watched young parents obsess over their baby's data set while never dreaming of looking into the crib. Naturally, once the more elaborate option is available, the eager young parent is compelled to do all the monitoring they can in the name of care.

Children raised in such a nervous climate can have little experience of true solitude, even in sleep. And as they grow up they'll find that becoming lost or finding oneself in a strange place is a panicky experience. The media historian James Gleick takes all this to its most essential, umbilical level when he notes, "We were born connected. Solitude came with maturity."[95] But in place of solitude's maturity, we seem to now halt at every unknown and beg our devices to locate both loved ones and ourselves. Wherever we go in the world, or in life, we are known and held in the cradle of some server. Which of the earth's 197 million square miles do you occupy? This one, right here.

For companies like Google and Facebook, such self-tracking remains crucial; they will not happily allow you to go through your life without a preserving trace of your movements and actions and thoughts. The Germans have a term for the record that so doggedly follows us through our screen age lives: *digitale Schleimspur*—digital slime. The record of your life trails behind you in an unbreakable excretion of data. Google CEO Eric Schmidt famously responded to critics of such slime by suggesting, "If you have something that you don't want anyone to know, maybe you shouldn't be doing it in the first place."[96] Of course, he was assuming that citizens should always "be good." And he did not go into the minutiae of who gets to determine what "being good" looks like (nor whether outlaw individuals like Edward Snowden may be "good" and "evil" at the same time).

In Dave Eggers's not so far-fetched novel *The Circle*, going off-grid becomes a pseudo-crime, and those who attempt to disappear are ruthlessly hunted down. The novel's climax is a manhunt performed by a swarm of camera-equipped drones. An audience of laughing tech workers watches on screens as a man is driven mad by their insistence that he be known and monitored. Using these drones—and an online crowd of helpers—the novel's heroine tracks down her secluded ex-boyfriend, Mercer, in the woods where he's attempting to live a disconnected life. He tries to escape in his truck, but the flock of metal beasts keeps up. Mae, the heroine, calls out through a drone's speakers:

> "Mercer. It's me, Mae! Can you hear me?"
>
> There was some faint sign of recognition on his face. He squinted, and looked toward the drone again, disbelieving. . . .

"Mercer!" she said, in mock-authoritative voice. "Mercer, stop the car and surrender. You're surrounded."[97]

Mercer is surrounded by "friends" who refuse to allow him to experience solitude. Ultimately, their insistence on monitoring has devastating consequences.

We're all hounded by monitoring systems, though it happens in less obvious ways outside of novels: when Facebook targets us with location-specific ads (and incorporates the faces of our friends into those ads); when we sigh and click "yes" to an app that wants to use our location data; when we allow ourselves to be tagged and tracked "for our own benefit." The Eggers vision is hardly speculative fiction at all. The freedoms of online life so easily bend toward the Orwellian.

We forget how new and unnatural this mania for tracking really is. Even the famous were relatively anonymous once. Charlie Chaplin, for example, is said to have entered a "Charlie Chaplin Lookalike" contest in 1921 and come in twentieth place—so vague was the public's idea of his face. In fact, it's estimated that the first fifteen presidents of the United States would have been unrecognizable to the average American.[98] Certainly Mark Twain's tale of the prince and the pauper—where the super-rich and super-poor swap places—is conceivable only in a world where people are free to wander beyond their set "brands." As the unacknowledged prince sits down with a family of peasants, Twain's narrator intones: "It does us all good to unbend sometimes."[99]

Real growth, real coming of age, demands such unbending, a loosening of borders—both the borders of our home and the borders of our identity—if only so that we may better understand where we come from. In plainer words: not 'til we are lost can we hope to be found.

Full-on dystopias aren't likely so long as we insist on being lost and untracked for some portion of our lives. So long as we respect the Mercers of the world. Only then, after all, do we reckon with the fact of our raw selves. How amazing—what an enormous relief!—to affirm that we exist whether others watch us or not. And what a relief to know that I'm more than the zeitgeist that has settled on my skin.

8

A Walk in the Wilds

On April 14, 1934, Richard Byrd went out for his daily walk. The air was the usual temperature: minus 57 degrees Fahrenheit. He stepped steadily through the drifts of snow, making his rounds. And then he paused to listen. Nothing.

He attended, a little startled, to the cloud-high and over-powering silence he had stepped into. For miles around the only other life belonged to a few stubborn microbes that clung to sheltering shelves of ice. It was only 4 p.m., but the land quavered in a perpetual twilight. There was—was there?—some play on the chilled horizon, some crack in the bruised Antarctic sky. And then, unaccountably, Richard Byrd's universe began to expand.

Later, back in his hut, huddled by a makeshift furnace, Byrd wrote in his diary:

Here were imponderable processes and forces of the cosmos, harmonious and soundless. Harmony, that was it! That was what came out of the silence—a gentle rhythm, the strain of a perfect chord, the music of the spheres, perhaps.

It was enough to catch that rhythm, momentarily to be myself a part of it. In that instant I could feel no doubt of man's oneness with the universe.[100]

Admiral Byrd had volunteered to staff a weather base near the South Pole for five winter months. But the reason he was there *alone* was far less concrete. Struggling to explain his reasons, Byrd admitted that he wanted "to know that kind of experience to the full . . . to taste peace and quiet and solitude long enough to find out how good they really are." He was also after a kind of personal liberty, for he believed that "no man can hope to be completely free who lingers within reach of familiar habits."[101]

Byrd received the Medal of Honor for his work, but for most of us, the choice to be alone in the wild is not rewarded at all; in fact it is highly suspect. A trek into nature is assumed to be proof of some anti-social tendency. A feral disposition. Our friends and families don't want us to wander off in search of the expansive, euphoric revelations that Byrd experienced in his Antarctic abyss. So we keep warm, instead, within our comfortable culture of monitoring and messaging. We abhor the disconnection that the woods, the desert, the glacier threaten us with in their heartless way. Our culture leans so sharply toward the social that those who wander into the wild are lucky if they're only considered weird. At worst, they're

Unabombers. The bias is so strong that we stop thinking about that wilderness trek altogether; besides, we tell ourselves, surely we aren't capable of such adventures. We'd wind up rotting in a ditch. And even if we *could* access the wild, we probably don't have the fine kind of soul that would get something out of it.

There *is* something dangerous about isolating oneself the way Admiral Byrd did. Mystic euphoria aside, he nearly died there at the frozen anchor of the world. His furnace began leaking carbon monoxide into his hut. Indeed, a company of men down at his base camp had to hike in and save him when his health deteriorated. Other solitaries without radio-handy companions have been markedly less lucky. Think of young Chris McCandless (memorialized in Jon Krakauer's book *Into the Wild*), who left no trail for his acquaintances when he hiked into the Alaskan wilderness with nothing but a rifle and a 10-pound bag of rice. After 119 days he died in the wilderness he had sought—poisoned by mouldy seeds is one guess—stranded, anyway, by the vagaries of Mother Nature.

In the final days of Admiral Byrd's solo Antarctic adventure—before men from his base camp came to rescue him—he was very close to death himself. Frostbite began to eat his body, and he mumbled like a monk in his sleeping bag, at times growing so weak he was unable to move. He cradled heat pads against himself and scraped lima beans from cans. He tried to play card games and was baffled by the weakness in his arms. He tried to read a biography of Napoleon but the words blurred and swam uselessly on the pages. "You asked for it," a small voice within him said. "And here it is."[102]

But despite all this trauma, Admiral Byrd was returned to society with a gift that society itself could never give him; he carried "something I had not fully possessed before," he wrote in his memoir. It was an "appreciation of the sheer beauty and miracle of being alive. . . . Civilization has not altered my ideas. I live more simply now, and with more peace."[103]

When Byrd and McCandless trekked into the wild, so doggedly insisting on solitude in nature, they both tapped into a human impulse that our progress has all but quashed.

I spoke with a bright teenager called Derrick who told me that, for him, communing with nature means first getting a friend to be the "designated texter." He let the phrase dangle there a moment.

At last I bit. "What's a designated texter?" His explanation was heartbreaking: Derrick and his friends are so inundated by messages from anxious parents that, in order to feel properly free when they go exploring, they are forced into a bit of trickery. Half a dozen phones will be left in the care of the "designated texter" (they take turns), and, free at last, the others will wander into the woods, or down to the beach, confident they won't be hassled for a few hours at least. The texter, left in a basement or bedroom with a movie to watch on a laptop, responds with neutral comments to parents who feel compelled to check in; the texter provides a banal assurance, which is all that's needed to grant the others some untethered recreation.

What struck me was not the deception, per se, but the way these youths (always depicted in the media as phone junkies) had engineered a disconnection into their lives. They weren't experiencing total solitude when they tramped off with their friends—but they were lowering their levels of connection, mediating things in order to experience an authenticity and communion with nature that their parents took for granted only a few decades earlier. And yet they could accomplish this only through subterfuge. They were like bandits forced to steal an encounter with the wild. While we talk about the rights of impoverished children to have access to the Internet, perhaps we need to also talk about their right to access nature.

Digital natives like Derrick live within a bizarre paradox. On the one hand, they spend their lives exploring territories that their parents could only dream of accessing: *Pterodactyl porn? Don't mind if I do.* But on the other hand they're physically constrained in the real world to a degree that would have left their parents bucking. In the United Kingdom, for example, the radius around a home that children freely wander in has shrunk by a stunning 90 per cent since 1970.[104] Richard Louv, author of *Last Child in the Woods*, has described an epidemic of "nature deficit disorder"—the human cost of alienation from nature—which includes "diminished use of the senses, attention difficulties, and higher rates of physical and emotional illnesses."[105] Stephen Moss, one of the U.K.'s leading nature writers, produced a report for the Nature Trust in which he insists this is "not an anachronistic lament on modernity" but rather an assertion of an inalienable right, a right to see things growing and peer into wide-open sky, a right to build a fire on the beach or hike a country trail with a sense of true autonomy from the usual authorities. It ought to be a right to walk out into the green and blue world.

When did we first step out of the wild and into the forever-crowded city? There was a time when all we had was access to nature—we were so inextricably in it and of it. Our ancestors spent their first 2.5 million years operating as nomadic groups that gathered plants where they grew and hunted animals where they grazed. Relatively recently, around ten thousand years ago, something phenomenal shifted: beginning in modern-day Turkey, Iran, and elsewhere in the Middle East, our ancestors embarked on what's called the Agricultural Revolution. They began to manipulate and care for plants (and animals), devoting their days to sowing seeds and battling weeds, leading herds to pastures and fighting off their predators. This was no overnight transformation; rather, bit by bit, these nomads reimagined nature as a force to be contained and managed.

Or was it nature, rather, that was doing the taming? Even as we domesticated the wheat, rice, and corn that we still rely on to feed ourselves, human lives were bent in servitude to the care of crops. The historian Yuval Noah Harari calls this exchange "history's biggest fraud" and argues that "the Agricultural Revolution left farmers with lives generally more difficult and less satisfying than those of foragers."[106]

The historian of food Margaret Visser agrees, calling rice, for example, a "tyrant" that

> governs power structures, technological prowess, population figures, interpersonal relationships, religious custom. . . . Once human beings agree to grow rice as a staple crop, they are caught in a web of consequences from which they cannot escape—if only because from that moment on rice dictates to them not only what they must do, but also what they prefer.[107]

Relying on single staples for the majority of one's caloric intake can be a gamble, too: even while it allows for exponential population growth, the diets of individuals become less varied and more vulnerable to attack by pests and blight. Others have pointed out that, just as domesticated animals have smaller brains than their wild ancestors, the brain of the "domesticated human" is significantly smaller than that of our pre-agriculture, pre-city selves.[108]

Meanwhile, the care of crops and animals required so much of humans that they were forced to cease their wandering ways and remain permanently beside their fields—and so we have wheat and its cousins to thank for the first human settlements.

Professor Harari notes that the plot of land around Jericho, in Palestine, would have originally supported "at most one roaming band of about a hundred relatively healthy and well-nourished people," whereas, post–Agricultural Revolution (around 8500 BCE), "the oasis supported a large but cramped village of 1,000 people, who suffered far more from disease and malnourishment."[109] The Middle East was, by then, covered with similar, permanent settlements.

By 7500 BCE, our disenfranchisement from nature was expressed more dramatically when the citizens of Jericho constructed an enormous wall around their city—the first of its kind. The purpose of this wall was probably twofold: it protected against floods as well as marauding enemies. What's extraordinary about this first significantly walled city is the almost fanatical determination to withdraw from that earlier, wild world. The wall, made of stone, was five feet thick and twelve feet tall. In addition, a ditch was constructed adjacent to the wall that was nine feet deep and almost thirty feet wide. Jericho's workers dug this enormous bulwark against the outside from solid bedrock—a feat of determined withdrawal that would have been unthinkable to our pre-agricultural ancestors. This was a true denial of the sprawling bushland that had been our home for millennia. The "wild" had been exiled. And we never invited it back. By the fourth century BCE the Agricultural Revolution had evolved into an "urban revolution"—one we are living out still.

In 2007, it was announced that more people live in cities than not. According to the World Health Organization, six out of every ten people will live in cities by 2030.[110] No reversal of the trend is in sight. And as the city continues to draw us to itself, like some enormous, concrete siren, we begin to convince ourselves that this crowded existence is the only "natural" life, that there is nothing for us beyond the walls of Jericho. Perhaps, goes the myth, there never was.

One day, we are told, Socrates was walking in a rural patch outside Athens and his companion turned to him, saying: "You, my remarkable friend, appear to be totally out of place. . . . As far as I can tell, you never even set foot beyond the city walls." Socrates replied: "Forgive me, my friend. I am devoted to learning; landscapes and trees have nothing to teach me—only the people in the city can do that."[111] Why does Socrates say this? Why does the philosopher brush aside "the wild" as though it were void of meaning? Perhaps he does not need to go looking for time with nature because ordinary life in the fifth century BCE threatened to flood with too much of that already. Nature and its dangers would have been forever banging at the door of his urban home, hungry to reclaim him. For the Greeks, the notion of being tossed away from civilization and back into the wild was a fundamental terror. *Eremia*—their word for both "solitude" and "wilderness"—was something that the wicked would be cast into.

The terror lasted for centuries, but slowly, ever so incrementally, the wilderness lost its deadly look. Once the wild is totally tamed, it becomes less a place of exile and more a place where one can return for some primal oneness with the universe. (The kind of communion Admiral Byrd envisioned.) By the eighteenth and nineteenth centuries, Europeans had largely got over their fear of becoming wolf meat. We find in the raptures of Goethe and Rousseau a transformation from *eremia* to appreciative depictions of the "sublime"—awesome landscapes that wait beyond our artificial, picturesque towns.

This sparking love for nature was fanned into full flame with the work of the Romantic poets. Here is William Wordsworth, for example, writing in 1798:

> One impulse from a vernal wood
> May teach you more of man,
> Of moral evil and of good,
> Than all the sages can.
>
> Sweet is the lore which Nature brings;
> Our meddling intellect
> Mis-shapes the beauteous forms of things:—
> We murder to dissect.[112]

When Rousseau opened *The Social Contract* with his famous decree "Man is born free and everywhere he is in chains," he assumed that if we could just *get back* to our primal, pre-city selves, all would be well. Rousseau would have had a rude awakening, though, if he were able to visit his contemporaries in North America, for whom wilderness had reverted to a dark place filled with "savages" and beasts. For the first white settlers in America, nature was a thing to be conquered, not appreciated. Indeed, the clichéd "nature lover" view of wilderness that took hold in Europe was a kind of luxury possible only because city-making and industrialization had insulated

Europeans from nature's dangers. Perhaps romantic characters like Goethe and Rousseau (and later, in America, John
Muir of the Sierra Club) fell in love with "the wild" because
they didn't have to fear it. Perhaps their flushed enthusiasms
are a warning sign that a more authentic, more dangerous
experience of nature has been stamped out.

Now, as the urban revolution reaches a head and humans become
more citified than not, "nature deficit disorder" blooms in every
apartment block, and the crowds of urbanity push out key
components of human life that we never knew we needed to
safeguard. Nature activists like Richard Louv use less poesy
and more research to prove that cities impoverish our sensory
experience and can lead to an impoverished identity, too—one
deprived of "the sense of humility required for true human
intelligence," as Louv puts it.[113]

But what really happens when we turn too often toward
society and away from the salt-smacking air of the seaside or
our prickling intuition of unseen movements in a darkening
forest? Do we really dismantle parts of our better selves?

A growing body of research suggests exactly that. A study
from the University of London, for example, found that members of the remote cattle-herding Himba tribe in Namibia,
who spend their lives in the open bush, had greater attention
spans and a greater sense of contentment than urbanized
Britons and, when those same tribe members moved into
urban centres, their attention spans and levels of contentment

dropped to match their British counterparts.[114] Dr. Karina Linnell, who led the study, was "staggered" by how superior the rural Himba were.[115] She told the BBC that these profound differences were "a function of how we live our lives," suggesting that overcrowded urban settings demand altered states of mind. Linnell even proposes that employers, were they looking to design the best workforces, consider stationing employees who need to concentrate outside the city.[116]

Meanwhile, at Stanford University, study participants had their brains scanned before and after walking in grassy meadows and then beside heavy car traffic. Participants walking in urban environments had markedly higher instances of "rumination"—a brooding and self-criticism the researchers correlated with the onset of depression. And, just as parts of the brain associated with rumination lit up on urban walks, they calmed down during nature walks.[117]

Photos of nature will increase your sense of affection and playfulness.[118] A quick trip into the woods, known as "forest bathing" in Japan, reduces cortisol levels and boosts the immune system.[119] Whether rich or poor, students perform better with access to green space.[120] And a simple view of greenery can insulate us from stress and increase our resilience to adversity.[121] Time in nature even boosts, in a very concrete way, our ability to smell, see, and hear. The data piles up.

The cumulative effect of all these benefits appears to be a kind of balm for the harried urban soul. In the nineteenth century, as urbanization began its enormous uptick, as overcrowded and polluted city streets became, in the words of Pip in *Great Expectations*, "all asmear with filth and fat and blood and foam," doctors regularly prescribed "nature" for the anxiety and depression that ailed their patients. The smoke and noise of cities were seen as truly foreign influences that required remedy in the form of nature retreats. Sanitariums were nestled in lush, Arcadian surrounds to counteract the disruptive influence of cities. Eva Selhub and Alan Logan, the authors of *Your Brain on Nature*, have described how these efforts gave way, in the twentieth century, to the miracle of pills, which allowed ill people to remain in the city indefinitely, so long as they took their medicine: "The half-page advertisement for the Glen Springs Sanitarium gave way to the full-page advertisement for the anti-anxiety drug meprobamate."[122] In this light, today's urban populace, which manages itself with sleeping pills and antidepressants (more than 10 per cent of Americans take antidepressants), may remind us of the soma-popping characters in Aldous Huxley's dystopian *Brave New World*. That vision may be changing at last, though. Today, as the curative effects of nature come back to light, some doctors have again begun prescribing "time outdoors" for conditions as various as asthma, ADHD, obesity, diabetes, and anxiety.[123]

Nature's benefits may still be given short shrift, though, because the online platforms that manage and guide so much of our lives do not benefit from promoting access to wilderness. Even the semi-enclosure of cities has become too "wild" a thing for some, and entire campuses have been designed in Silicon Valley where tech workers can eat, sleep, and play in a latter-day Jericho—a sanitized bubble. Google released new campus designs in 2015 that are literally visions of giant domed communities that can control the climate in their "outdoor" spaces.[124] Then, in 2016, Amazon began building three 100-foot-tall glass domes ("biospheres") outside their Seattle headquarters, in which employees can wander among endangered plant species while they brainstorm.[125]

But the wilderness, the wild, the true out-of-doors, is a place where we *hand over* our control. We become little bodies in a very big world and egos shrink accordingly. We may boast total control over our online avatars and Twitter feeds, but offline we manage only an infinitely small portion of the gears that run the universe. Matthew Crawford suggests that our online life is a place where we seem to have more impact, more agency, than we would normally deserve. Online gaming, gambling, and messaging systems produce a surety, what MIT's Natasha Dow Schüll calls "manufactured certainties," and (Crawford notes) "such pursuits help us manage the anxiety and depression that come when experiences of genuine agency are scarce."[126] Life online allows me to feel expansive, as though I am shinier and more attractive (certainly better spoken) than I am in real life. In contrast, the natural world—which hunkers above and around us, both sublime and ruthless—forces us into the opposite situation. Step from your Tumblr feed into the woods and you are demoted. Our agency inside an unfeeling and immobile landscape is puny. Out there, Crawford writes, the self "comes into view as being *in a situation* that is not of its own making."[127] Where the Internet says, "Here it is, here you go," the creaking woods say, "You cannot know. Only wonder . . . and wonder . . ."

We should not fear the wondering. To walk out of our houses and beyond our city limits is to shuck off the pretense and assumptions that we otherwise live by. This is how we open ourselves to brave new notions or independent attitudes. This is how we come to know our own minds.

For some people, a brief walk away from home has been the only respite from a suffocating domestic life. Think of an English woman in the early nineteenth century with very few activities open to her—certainly few chances to escape the confines of the drawing room. In *Pride and Prejudice*, Elizabeth Bennet's determination to walk in the countryside signals her lack of convention. When her sister Jane takes ill at the wealthy Mr. Bingley's house, Elizabeth traipses alone through fields of mud to be with her, prompting Bingley's sister to call her "wild" in appearance with hair that has become unpardonably "blowsy": "That she should have walked three miles so early in the day, in such dirty weather, and by herself, was almost incredible . . . they held her in contempt for it."[128] Throughout the novel, Elizabeth runs into rude yet winning Mr. Darcy while out on her solitary rambles ("she felt all the perverseness of the mischance that should bring him where no one else was brought"[129]). In these scenes, Elizabeth walks beyond the borders of her class and transgresses the limits of propriety.

Each time society's demands encroach on her, she instinctively seeks the release and independence of a walk into fields and over hills. Why should this be? Perhaps because wilderness is the only place where she can think for herself. An empty drawing room isn't enough; she needs to move. Not in a stuffy carriage but of her own accord and at her own pace. I think Elizabeth Bennet would lament the loss of such rambles— those steady, three-miles-an-hour steps. She really requires a few acres of honest dirt road or scraggly moor to parse out her own position.

The philosopher Thomas Hobbes had a walking stick with an inkhorn built into its top so he could jot things down as they popped into his head during long walks. Rousseau would have approved of the strategy; he writes, "I can only meditate when I am walking. When I stop, I cease to think; my mind only works with my legs." Albert Einstein, for his part, was diligent about taking a walk through the woods on the Princeton campus every day. Other famous walkers include Charles Dickens and Mother Teresa, John Bunyan and Martin Luther King Jr., Francis of Assisi and Toyohiko Kagawa. Why do so many bright minds seem set on their walks away from the desk? It can't be just that they need a break from thinking—some of their best thinking is done *during* this supposed "downtime" out of doors.

In educational circles, there is a theory that helps explain the compulsion; it's called the theory of loose parts. Originally developed by architect Simon Nicholson in 1972, when he was puzzling over how to make playgrounds more engaging, the loose parts theory suggests that one needs random elements, changing environments, in order to think independently and cobble together one's own vision of things. Nature is an infinite source of loose parts, whereas the office or the living room, being made by people, is limited. Virginia Woolf noted that even the stuff and furniture of our homes may "enforce the memories of our own experience" and cause a narrowing, a suffocating effect. Outside of our ordered homes, though, we escape heavy memories about the way things have always been and become open to new attitudes.

But there does seem to be an art to walks; we must work at making use of those interstitial moments. Going on a hike, or even just taking the scenic route to the grocery store, is a chance to dip into our solitude—but we must seize it. If we're compelled by our more curious selves to walk out into the world—sans phone, sans tablet, sans Internet of Everything—then we still must decide to taste the richness of things.

Outside the maelstrom of mainstream chatter, we at last meet not just the bigger world but also ourselves. Confirmed flâneur William Hazlitt paints the picture well. When he wanders out of doors he is searching for

> liberty, perfect liberty, to think, feel, do, just as one pleases. . . . I want to see my vague notions float like the down on the thistle before the breeze, and not to have them entangled in the briars and thorns of controversy. For once, I like to have it all my own way; and this is impossible unless you are alone.[130]

This is the gift of even a short, solitary walk in a city park. To find, in glimpsing a sign of the elements, that one does belong to something more elemental than an urban crowd. That there is a universe of experience beyond human networks and social grooming—and that this universe is our true home. Workers in the cramped centre of Osaka may cut through Namba Park on their way to work; Torontonians may cut through Trinity Bellwoods Park on their way to the city's best bookshop; New Yorkers may cut through Central Park on their way to the Metropolitan Museum; and Londoners may cut through Hyde Park on their way to Royal Albert Hall. Stepping off the narrow sidewalk for even a few minutes, we may come across a new (and very old) definition of ourselves, one with less reference to others.

Kenny and I arrived at the scrubbed shoreline of Prince Edward Island and walked out onto the miles-long beach of Cavendish. The sand was deserted except for us. In two more weeks it'd be tourist season and sunscreen-polished families would lounge everywhere. But that day the scene was shockingly empty and washed-out, like a postcard from an Edwardian traveller.

We'd flown there at the end of May, not realizing the quiet Canadian island, flung partway into the Atlantic, would still be recovering from winter. They'd had eighteen feet of snow that year—so said the grocer, the lobsterman, the hotel clerk—and it had only just melted. Even as we rolled up our trousers and wandered onto the beach, pieces of ice were bobbing offshore.

We watched the pewter pattern of the waves awhile. We hiked past disintegrating red-clay cliffs toward dunes of sand stripped bare on one side by the tide's wind and furred on the other with hip-high grasses. Kenny said the steep slant of the dunes looked like the edge of an enormous pie, pressed up by a giant's thumb. The branches of nearby firs were like the arms of frightened old men, grey and scored by endless gales, flung inland.

Back in Toronto, we'd been living in a single room, a five-hundred-square-foot apartment near the city centre where we were constantly in each other's way. Every morning I pulled an old piano bench into the middle of the space and made it my writing desk. Every night we sat on the floor to eat our dinners. So we were a little drunk on the wide-open miles of Cavendish. We raced each other to the top of the dunes, nearly running in place as sand tracked beneath our feet. At the top we collapsed and saw where something close to sandstone had compressed, then crumbled; striations made by years of tides were revealed in cross-section. It was a miniature, organic architecture—the cliff-carved city of Petra. Our talk slowed, our steps drifted; we became lost in our separate worlds. Then Kenny wandered toward a pond beyond the dunes and I was utterly alone. Something about the ocean's blurred horizon and the freshly minted sand made the sensation a powerful one. *Nobody is watching you now.*

When did I last feel so happily cut off? It had been— yes—years. I'd lived in squashed little apartments; I'd shuffled onto subway cars. I'd worked in cafés and eaten with friends

at clattering restaurants where one shouts and nods, half hear-
ing the conversation. But now this wide-open ocean. It was
only a little reprieve, of course—and I knew Kenny was just
beyond the dunes—and yet I'd not felt so totally set apart from
the red-faced world in ages.

The natural world is invested with its own awful, sym-
bolic utterance. It invests our lives with meaning that we
cannot find among the crowdings of the metropolis. Look in
a river and we see Time rushing away; observe a favourite oak
sprouting new greenery and we flush with fresh hope for our
own renewal. In the infinitude of nature a solace and truth is
projected for us, reflecting and making sensible all the shifting
traumas and quandaries that roughen our lives. And so, as I
watched the waves, the infinite surety of their work, I ingested
some of their calm, their sanity.

But it hit me, barefoot in the sand: If being alone and
happy requires a beach wiped clean of footprints, if solitude
requires miles and miles of empty waves, then my real, non-
vacationing life is a lost cause. No, I needed to pack this sensation back to my regular days and keep it going in the city. It is
only for heroes like Admiral Byrd to spend months braving the
blistering extremes of the South Pole. The rest of us must benefit from braving the small, unpeopled corners of our little
lives, those corners of green we can dodge across. Heroes or
unknowns, we each have a date to keep in the wild—a date
with the world-altering, mind-blowing companion that is the
solitary self.

———

Having really un-citied ourselves and felt the bracing effects of nature, we emerge prepared to discover the last of solitude's benefits: the way it can, paradoxically, connect us to each other. In his essay collection *What Are People For?*, Wendell Berry describes a solitary walk in nature this way:

> One's inner voices become audible. One feels the attraction of one's most intimate sources.
>
> In consequence, one responds more clearly to other lives. The more coherent one becomes within oneself as a creature, the more fully one enters into the communion of all creatures.[131]

When Kenny came around the dune he found me shirtless and comically staring. Don't forget, I told myself as we turned back. Don't forget Cavendish. As we walked toward the cottage, an easy mile, I dug a stone from my pocket and handed it to Kenny; and he had one for me.

Part IV

Knowing Others

I hold this to be the highest task for a bond between two people: that each protects the solitude of the other.

—*Rainer Maria Rilke*

9

Social Stories

When I walk into Keith Oatley's office at the University of Toronto I notice a worn volume of Virginia Woolf's *Three Guineas* resting on his desk—the sort of book that smells faintly of almonds and damp. Oatley's liver-spotted hand strays to its cover as he says hello, and I have the lumpish impression that I've interrupted.

Oatley is seventy-five years old and possessed of a prickly intellect, a cragged brow, and bushy caterpillar eyebrows that he uses to punctuate his remarks. He is both a novelist and a professor emeritus of cognitive psychology; it's this rare combination of interests that has drawn me here—Oatley has devoted much of his life to understanding what happens in the mind as we read.

I've come with a particular question in mind and, sitting opposite Oatley, in the student's chair, I try to map it out. Proust once defined reading as "that fruitful miracle of a communication in the midst of solitude."[132] I explain that I want to better understand what that means. How and why do we communicate "in the midst of solitude"? What does that detachment change about the kinds of messages we receive from books? And what exactly is the "fruitful miracle" that a reader's withdrawal makes possible? "What," I say at last, "was Proust talking about?"

Oatley glances out the window and says, "Reading is very different from our day-to-day life, isn't it?" This seems a little obvious, and for a few seconds I worry he'll stop there. But then he clicks onward, tapping one hand in the palm of the other. "When we read, we can become people who we are not. A metaphorical process occurs. One's self becomes Elizabeth Bennet or Anna Karenina. One becomes a fictional protagonist. We can live more lives than our own." If Woolf had been able to speak from that copy of *Three Guineas* on the table, she might have chimed in with something she once wrote in a letter to Ethel Smyth: "the state of reading consists in the complete elimination of the ego."[133] People talk about getting "lost" in books, and I suppose this is what they mean— that the fortress we build around ourselves, the pretense of a single "self" that protects us as we shuffle through our days, begins to crumble ten pages into a good novel, letting a new voice, a new identity, wash over us.

When I read Nabokov's *Lolita* and spend a few days taking on the voice of a pedophile and murderer, or when I read Wharton's *The House of Mirth* and get some glimpse of what it means to be a woman enduring the limitations of a misogynist society, these are gifts of experience. But those gifts can be received only when I quiet myself, calm my otherwise feverish ego. This process—the solitary giving over of the mind—is something that readers train themselves to do over the course of years. But eventually they develop a talent for it, and then they begin to nurture something that we need much more of—empathy. The constant reader, says Oatley, learns to hold opinions and ideas that are not their own. We become primed not just to *discover* new thoughts but to *live* them, absorb them, care about them. Others, like York University psychologist Raymond Mar, have done the MRI scans to back Oatley up.[134] The parts of the brain that are involved in reading fiction in particular share large areas with the parts of the brain that help us understand other people in daily life. When we read, our brains behave as though we are experiencing what the hero experiences. The solitary reader rehearses the lives of others. And I think that must be the definition of empathy—to rehearse the lives of others.

But that solitary reading experience is now endangered, and so is the empathy it fosters. Our stories are going social. We can assume that, in thirty years, readers and writers will use platform technologies to constantly interact with and shape each other, for better or worse. Authors will enlist crowd-sourcing and artificial intelligence to help them write their stories. (Indeed, I know an author who has launched an app specifically designed to allow her fans to collaborate on ideas for her upcoming books.)[135] These same authors will mostly earn their salaries as performers and brands. Already, in the non-fiction world, many authors see books as reverse-engineered TED Talks—you write the book as a calling card. Books themselves will exist only rarely as stand-alone items; they'll usually be cross-promotional products, merged with apps and games, songs and TV. (I note that today's non-fiction bestseller is a Harry Potter colouring book for adults.) Our book choices will be partly determined by the catalogues of whatever platform we subscribe to. And the stories we read will not be static strings of text but, rather, will morph to accommodate personal preferences (the hero's race and sexuality will shift to your liking). Current trends will be subbed in, too: pop songs, cocktail choices, and the name of the president will all be dynamic elements in narratives that serve as echoes of an eternal present rather than time capsules of the past.

We're already primed for such a social reading experience. More than half of e-book buyers read their purchases on smartphones, and the number who read books "primarily" on their phones rose from 9 per cent in 2012 to 14 per cent in 2015.[136] When we do our book reading on the very devices that we use to connect to our social circles, we come to expect constant commenting and interjection. This is about more than just attention spans. It is perhaps not surprising that a Dartmouth College study released in 2016 found that, even when we focus on a text while using digital platforms, our focus becomes weighted toward the consumption of concrete details and away from the kinds of higher-level interpretation that imbue text with fuller meanings; of three hundred participants, those reading on digital platforms became mark-edly less able to draw inferences or think abstractly.[137] So, even if one could shut off alerts and messaging apps, the social device itself may remain a poor instrument for deep reading. Maryanne Wolf, a neuroscientist at Tufts University who spe-cializes in the reading brain, has argued that our smartphones are in fact "antithetical to deep reading."[138]

By contrast, readers and writers who know how to sit alone in a sustained way, those who know how to do that magic trick of dissolving into another person's selfhood, are begin-ning to look like wizards—or dinosaurs.

Books by Tolstoy and Proust, whatever their glowing aura, are increasingly viewed as a mere by-product of a par-ticular moment in technological history when, frankly, people didn't have other ways of entertaining themselves. *Sure,* the nineteenth-century dowager shrugs, *I guess I'll sit in this chair by the fire for the next eight hours.* Despite the success of some hefty tomes that have appeared during the age of screens (*The Goldfinch*, *The Luminaries*), some argue we're witnessing the last gasp of an outdated technology, that we should abandon those solitary storytelling devices (meaning books) and instead accept that meaning comes to us not through long, mono-lithic progressions of text but from the discovery of many voices, continually commenting on and reshaping each other. *Wired* magazine's founding executive editor, Kevin Kelly, has bemoaned the way books are "isolated items, independent from one another."[139] And media scholar Clay Shirky believes we're at the point where people are just pretending to love

Tolstoy and Proust because they think they're supposed to. *War and Peace* is "too long, and not so interesting." Those relics "were just a side-effect of living in an environment of impoverished access." And now we've moved past them toward "the greatest expansion of expressive capability the world has ever known."[140] The rhetoric reminds me of another technological intrusion, this one from the fourth millennium BCE.

Writing, when it first appeared, was a powerfully disruptive technology.[141] And for traditional reading to prosper, it needed us to adopt a very alien mental state. Berkeley psychologist Alison Gopnik has described how the invention of writing had to "hijack" parts of the brain that once were devoted to vision and speech.[142] Meanwhile, disorders like dyslexia highlight the fact that our brains can easily find such hijacking awkward or untenable. "In terms of human evolution," says Maryanne Wolf, "the brain was never meant to read."[143] And so, when you learned to parse meaning from these tiny black squiggles here, your brain jury-rigged circuits between regions designed for other purposes. But if reading is not "natural," why do we now do it with such fierce regularity? What was the big trade we got in exchange for this dramatic rerouting of our mental faculties?

When words are written down they become static, they lose the chaos and dynamism of plain talk. We trade that dynamism for something new—the sequence, the powerfully seductive structure of the written page. Written text allows for craftsmanship and deeper care—in both the creation and the reception of our ideas. It allows for complicated thoughts that would spin away into the breeze in a preliterate world. Oxford's star neurophysiologist Susan Greenfield argues that literary thought is, in fact, a magnification of thought itself: "As I see it, this idea of sequence is the very quintessence of a thought, and it is the mental step needed that will distinguish a line or train of thought from a one-off instantaneous emotion captured in a shriek of laughter or a scream."[144] Books stretch the reach of our thought sequences; they grant us superhuman abilities, pumping the brain up to giddy heights.

We easily forget how artificial, how steroidal, that boost really is. The ordered, sequential look of a book includes dozens of precise conventions, a set of invisible buttresses that our literary world relies on. Ancient texts called *scriptura continua*, for example, had no spaces between the words—it was expected that the written page would be used only as a reminder, a cheat sheet, for the *real* moment when the sounds of words were spoken aloud. Other little tools for making sense of the written page, like capital letters, punctuation marks, and the indenting of new paragraphs, are further inventions that began to show up as the written word broke away from the oral tradition and staked out its own, more solitary domain.

All these conventions eventually facilitated an almost trance-like experience, something Marshall McLuhan described as "our cinematic chase from left to right."[145] At full power, a good book trains us to forgo our immediate environment, trains us to sink into an imaginary space where its private life can thrive at the exclusion of all else. And, importantly, as we separate ourselves from the world around us, we connect to something larger and far away—something foreign.

This miracle of solitary connection must have been truly weird for those who first encountered it. Medieval readers were confused when they first saw people reading silently. It was bizarre to refrain from speaking the text out loud, to keep it bottled up inside. If you could travel back in time and watch a typical medieval reader sitting with a book, he would appear to you like a child, mouthing out the words as he went, jabbing his finger at each stubborn inch of text.[146] Even the sophisticated St. Augustine was startled when he first saw someone read silently. He takes the time in his *Confessions* to describe how the Bishop Ambrose scans his books without moving his lips; it was amazing that "his heart sought out the meaning" while his mouth didn't make a noise. This was a seductive new form of secrecy.

By the tenth century, silent, solitary reading had become more common.[147] And, via this silent retreat into the self, the reader also crept into a new, private arena for human thought. But that arena, again, was only the result of one technological reality. However common it became, there was never anything natural about the solitary reading culture that emerged over the following centuries, never anything natural about the tools for empathy it provided. Today, platform technologies undo the solitude once intrinsic to literary storytelling, and we must search to see if they undo our empathy, too.

———

"*Just because he can't love you the way you want him to doesn't mean he doesn't love you with everything he has.*" Twenty-four-year-old Anna Todd used her elbows to steer a grocery cart down the fluorescent-scorched aisles of Target. That way she could type on her Android phone as she rolled. Her thumbs darted and dodged across its glass surface. "*We are so completely different and yet the same.*" It would be a bestseller, the novel she was writing. It would touch the hearts of millions. "*I am a moth to his flame, and he never hesitates to burn me.*"

It really would, though—be a bestseller. It would be one of the biggest deals in publishing that nobody in publishing saw coming. Todd's chapters, which she posted on the go, via a social platform for amateur writers called Wattpad, would ultimately be downloaded more than one billion times. A can of food gets popped in the cart, a pack of batteries. "*I need him to not think of himself as a monster.*" The chapter was finished and Todd posted it while waiting in line at the till. Already she could feel the responses rolling in—hundreds, thousands of them—the suggestions for plot twists, the corrections and advice, the uptick in view counts and cascading streams of praise. Her book was a global phenomenon and she had not even finished writing it.

Todd was always a consummate fangirl. When she was thirteen, living in Dayton, Ohio, and dreaming of anywhere else, it was Josh Hartnett who obsessed her. Then it was *Twilight*. And then *Fifty Shades of Grey*. By eighteen she had married her high school boyfriend, a soldier whose work took the couple to Fort Hood, in Texas. There, Todd waitressed at a Waffle House, worked a bit at a makeup counter, and read her favourite fanfic online. By 2013, she was searching for work again and, perhaps out of boredom, the lamp of her attention swerved toward British boy band One Direction—specifically toward the group's shaggy-haired heartthrob, Harry Styles.

What set Todd apart from an everyday fangirl was the depth of her regard. She took to reading micro pieces of fan fiction—called imagines—that sometimes are used as captions for photos posted on Instagram. These imagines then led Todd to Wattpad, where many of the same writers were fleshing out their fantasies into full-blown works of fiction. The platform has a casting feature so that writers, rather than fully describing their characters, can simply "cast" a celebrity in the role. Harry Styles is a popular choice for male heroes (Taylor Swift is a favourite for heroines). In one popular take, he is involved in a human trafficking ring dealing in female sex slaves; in another, a vampire version of Styles steals a five-minute-old girl that he knows will become his "mate." (In most variations, Styles is darkly attracted to a helpless young girl who ultimately returns his desire.)

The story that Anna Todd began to write, called *After*, was in many respects a classic Wattpad fantasy: boy with tattoos must be tamed by the love of a good woman. Naughty Harry Styles meets virginal Tessa Young at Washington State University. He's awful. He drinks scotch and makes her cry. Yet his magnetism cannot be denied. Soon he is transformed by Tessa's love into his true, noble self. They're lying in the grass, the clean green grass, and Harry's holding himself over her, push-up style. It's all very tempting but he refuses to take her virginity until she's ready. "I feel as though I am ice and he is fire," muses Tessa.

When Wattpad's head of content, Ashleigh Gardner, noticed that Todd's downloads were tracking into the tens of millions, she thought it prudent to drop her a line. She asked Todd if she would be interested in allowing Wattpad to serve as her agent; would she like Wattpad to sell her work to a bona fide publisher? Todd didn't return the email for days, as the notion sounded "not real." But Wattpad did eventually convince her, and then sold the work to Simon & Schuster for six figures—with Wattpad taking their cut. And presto: the story became a series of four hard-copy novels now sold in thirty countries. Paramount has purchased the film rights.

How? How did this happen? I—the pretentious and old-fashioned scribe, who believes in MFAs and agents and agoraphobic writers in coffee-stained bathrobes—stand on the sidelines and wonder. Todd's prose is spontaneous—more like a chat session than traditional literature. Truman Capote's comment on Kerouac's *On the Road* comes to mind: "That's not writing; that's just typing." If literary writing is a way to assemble, by accretion, more than can be produced by our spontaneous mental processes, then *After* cannot really be called literature at all. It is the result of an automatic, pseudo-oral process. It's gossipy, highly sexed, and parsed into bite-sized morsels. And it has been extraordinarily successful.

After is native to the technological reality of its author. Todd explains her success this way: "People spend ten years trying to get a book published, they have degrees, they're a hell of a lot smarter than me, and they may have way better grammar than me. But I used the Internet, and that's what set me apart."[148]

As I learned more about Todd's work, and the platform on which she rocketed to stardom, I began to wonder whether I had somehow missed the boat. Had the real style by which storytelling works in the twenty-first century developed far from the place where I lived? Was I left, luggage in hand, waving from the dock? New forms of social storytelling meant authors and readers had more codependent relationships. It seemed old literary models where writers and readers exist only in their solitary silos were being torn down.

Wattpad bills itself as YouTube for readers. It allows anyone to post and download fiction free of charge. The platform's users are mostly young (78 per cent are under twenty-five years old) and women (making up a three-to-one ratio with men). They are also overwhelmingly participants in some form of fandom, writing and reading alternate tales based on *Game of Thrones* or *Harry Potter*, etc. There are fanfics about brands (*The Fault in Our Starbucks*); there is crossover fiction (*Pirates of the Caribbean* meets *Rocky Horror*); there is work based on runaway Internet memes (for example, *Alex from Target*, the global obsession that began when a cute Texan department store clerk was photographed by a customer); and even fiction based on apps (in one Kafkaesque example, Kim Kardashian becomes *Trapped in Her Own Game*). Wattpad writers publish their stories episodically, with short chapters uploaded as they're written. Once a chapter is posted, the website sends push notifications to alert readers. Readers then comment on the story's progress, enthuse about who's hot and who's "a slut," and point out plot holes for the author to correct. Typos and grammar problems are glossed over—a necessary indulgence. The writing is responsive, almost collaborative.

I managed to speak with Todd just as *After* was being shipped (in hard-copy form) to bookshops around the world, and I asked how it felt to be published on paper for a change. She told me, "It's so strange to have only one editor. I'm used to having thousands of editors, you know? I'm used to spending a couple hours just reading comments after I post something—and those comments would help me make the story better—but working with the editor from Simon & Schuster, there's just this weird silence when I send him something. I'm used to getting at least a 'yay' from readers right away."

Around this time, I had my chance to be a social writer, too. A tech company asked me to create a story for an app they were developing that would be "sort of a choose-your-own-adventure." Users would progress through the story by reading text messages, which then required a text back to "the narrator." Depending on what the reader typed, the story could fork in a dozen directions. The app picks up on likely key words in the reader's texts, so readers learn to eschew nuanced or creative responses. Out of morbid interest, I attempted to oblige the startup.

On opening their writing platform, I encountered a black screen and a set of tools. I could create boxes of "content" (i.e., story) and links between these boxes; each link would be triggered by key words in the text responses of readers. I looked over a seven-page set of instructions on how to use the program—full of advice like "use generic phrases" and "make your choices obvious." I wrote an opener box, which ended with a yes/no question and branched into two storylines; these storylines then subdivided into four more. Now I had four separate stories—except I only had one that I intended to tell. I stopped. I stared. It was as though all the words on my screen were swimming, devolving. And the only thing I was sure of was that this branch of social writing was not merely a new "style;" it was a new craft altogether. And my attitude toward storytelling was now all wrong.

I visited the plush headquarters of Wattpad, to see for myself a place where social writing was having some success. The space, near Toronto's downtown waterfront, is both thrown-together and glamorous, a mix of beanbag chairs and specially painted walls covered in dry-erase brainstorming residue. "We do, of course, have the obligatory tech-startup Ping-Pong table," said the charming communications specialist who greeted me. The desks, though, were almost entirely empty. "There are usually people here," the specialist assured me. I told her it was impressive to think how their staff of only one hundred could touch so many users in the age of platform technologies. Forty million users publish stories on the site (sans paycheque) and download them (sans payment). All told, folk spend nine billion minutes a month on Wattpad, consuming stories written in fifty languages. That number will be grievously out of date by the time you read this, though, since twenty-four hours of new reading material are posted there every second.

The site's co-founder, Allen Lau, met me in a room called My Wattpad Love.* He's a cheerful, slim, and bespectacled man, almost giddily optimistic. Since reading *Moby-Dick* on his phone in 2007, he has believed that mobile and social technology is the future of storytelling, and he reaches near-evangelical tones when discussing his work. "We're doing something quite Internet native here," he told me. "The stories have become interactive." So interactive, in fact, that authors have begun to create dummy Wattpad accounts for their fictional characters—allowing them to join the conversation in the comment forum. Commentary pours into narrative, and narrative backsplashes into commentary.

Another innovation on Wattpad is the way Lau has monetized things. Advertisements for the launch of the movie

---

* The rooms at Wattpad HQ are each named after popular Wattpad stories. "My Wattpad Love" is a romance by Ariana Godoy about a girl who finds a sense of community by publishing stories on Wattpad, but then encounters a cocky Wattpad user who smokes and is mean to her. She is drawn to his damaged soul and they fall in love.

The Fault in Our Stars, for example, were directed toward readers who clicked on tear-jerker romance stories that Wattpad had commissioned to serve as bait for *Fault*'s demographic. Meanwhile, in the Philippines, where the platform is particularly popular, Unilever sponsors content about young people who may or may not use Unilever products. (A television mini-series called *Wattpad Presents* is produced in the Philippines, too; it brings to life popular Wattpad love stories.) "Five years ago if you didn't tell consumers that a story was sponsored they'd get very upset," said Lau. "But five years from *now* it may simply be expected. And at the end of the day, if the consumer is not bombarded with advertising, maybe it's okay."

While Wattpad, like all platform companies, has found ways to monetize the labour of unpaid users, Lau believes that it also provides genuine benefits to would-be writers. "In the old model, with traditional publishing, people had to complete an entire book before getting feedback. Then you'd have to wait to get an agent, wait for an editor. There were all these gatekeepers." Lau gives me an open and guileless smile. "The Internet has provided a new option for writers. I think it's a powerful option. And the future of storytelling is very different."

Perhaps, given how different this future is, it's not surprising that conventional publishing is still not something Anna Todd aspires to. Despite her enormous success, she plans to continue writing on the Wattpad platform. Far from begrudging the lack of payment, Todd is so enamoured with Wattpad that she feels uncomfortable writing with more solitary media like Microsoft Word. "It's weird not to write on

Wattpad," she told me. "Even writing a new epilogue for one of the Simon & Schuster books, I had to work on the Wattpad platform. It's weird." She is convinced that Word is a little defunct, in fact, like a typewriter or roll of papyrus. "I definitely think all writing will be like this in the future," she told me. "That fourth wall between the author and the reader doesn't need to be there."

Things were still foggy. To understand the social writing experience, I'd have to also look at the social *reading* experience—the two were working in tandem. So I got to know Bob Stein, whose scope of vision in these matters is difficult to overstate. Stein is a seventy-year-old New Yorker who, for thirteen years, led the development of the Criterion film collection. He was the one who first saw that the true glory of a film library like Criterion's is its ability to stuff a laserdisc or DVD with hours and hours of marginalia. Deleted scenes could be restored and, more importantly, directors could lace their films with commentary (Criterion movies were the first to include scene-by-scene audio commentaries). Consumers wanted access to conversation *around* the film. It was a brilliant move, and one that tapped into the nascent tug of social grooming. When Martin Scorsese chats about the making of *Goodfellas* in a tone that's directed *right at you*, you feel empowered and connected to a Hollywood that once was coolly aloof.

Stein's new foray into commentary is far more social. These days he is director of the Institute for the Future of the Book, which is mandated to influence "the evolution of new forms of intellectual expression and discourse."[149] Key among these: their SocialBook platform allows any reader to comment in the margins of digital texts and chat with a community that lives in those margins. It's a sort of live and permanent book club—one with massive ramifications once properly deployed.

"Until people *try* social reading, they simply don't get it," Stein told me. "Especially for a generation raised on solo reading, it's like explaining sex to a six-year-old. It doesn't *sound* like it's going to be much fun." I lob at him the old notion of the solitary reader, curled up somewhere by a fire, but Stein bats it away. "People *think* they want to be alone on the page, but once you've had the experience of seeing how commentary can enrich your understanding—I'm telling you, this changes everything. It's deeply experiential.

"Nobody is going to want to read alone," Stein continued. "The affordances of electronic reading are going to get increasingly interesting. Print books may have a future—but only as art objects. And, as reading goes social, the collaborative effort will be fun and productive."

At the prestigious Dalton School in Manhattan's Upper East Side, Sol Gaitán has been teaching her Hispanic literature class using a SocialBook prototype for the past three years. Gaitán is herself a solitary person; she loves reading paper versions of books and shuns platforms like Facebook. Yet she now calls herself a pioneer of the social reading movement. When I spoke with her she'd been reading *Don Quixote* (unabridged, and in the original seventeenth-century Spanish) with a class of three Dalton seniors. Her students were reading the thousand-page book exclusively on screens. They left a trail of comments in the digital margins as they went.

"At first they didn't want to," Gaitán told me. "They were annoyed because the program kept sending them alerts whenever anybody commented on the text. But soon they saw this was just like the social media they were already using. Like texting or Twitter." Gaitán notes that SocialBook also makes it more difficult for students to fake a reading experience, since it maintains a record of your progress—all those comments become bread crumbs, proving a reader was there.

In the last few centuries, "reading may have become a solitary act," Gaitán told me, "but it was more public when books weren't so common, when they were read aloud to a group. So, in a way, we are going back in time. We're back to the idea of sitting around and listening to a reader. It's very much like going back to orality. And I suspect that, just as everything is now becoming social, reading will become quite social with time." Gaitán finds the process personally thrilling, not just a handy teaching tool: "I used to write in the margins of my book, and those thoughts would just go back on my bookshelf. But now I write in the margins of a digital book and it can be shared. This feels like a very important thing."

Meanwhile, I was still trying to craft a story for that startup. Reader feedback in that case was not just "a very important thing;" it was fundamental to the story's progression. But I couldn't wrap my mind around the premise—a dozen dramatic arcs (any one of which can intersect with all the others) leading eventually to a dozen different endings, all contingent on the feelings and reactions of the unknown reader—to say nothing of the algorithm's own predilections.

Why, I wondered, would I work on the text in these threads with any real effort if readers were only going to read 10 per cent of them at most? Social storytelling was making me slough off my sentences—it was making me care less about the craft of my writing. I was amazed, if not exactly surprised, to see how a switch in medium could change my attitude so sharply.

Back in 1997, Sun Microsystems studied how people read and write online and found that it bore little resemblance to the quaint approach that's historically thought of as "reading" and "writing." Only 16 per cent of people read web pages the way they read books, for example. The majority "read" the page by scanning it, bouncing from corner to corner and picking out phrases and images in a hunter-gatherer fashion. Jakob Nielsen, the study's author, described how people read online this way: "They don't."[150]

To accommodate the new medium's slippery quality, content creators were encouraged to create text that was always scannable, concise, and objective—with bulleted lists and a maximum of one idea per paragraph. Since then, improvements to the usability of online text have been made, but these represent our bowing to the medium and not the reverse.

We did not simply move our old reading habits online. We abbreviated our words, we highlighted ourselves, hyperlinked ourselves. By 2010, researchers found that we'd learned to focus mainly on previews and subject headings in emails.[151] We digitized what had been an analogue approach to thinking. Then, marketers and publishers were encouraged by experts to consider that an increasing portion of their consumers would be reading content on mobile technology, so text should be further abbreviated and simplified to accommodate miniature screens and on-the-go attention spans—we learned to truncate, to make our reading as efficient and piecemeal as possible. Naturally, such a radical streamlining of the reading experience also made the content far, far more shareable. The way had been paved for Lau's new forms of social storytelling.

As our social impulse makes its way back to the surface, the technological determinists among us argue that another Gutenberg-scale shift in our story-lives is inevitable. The SocialBooks and Anna Todds of the world are our first glimpses of a new/old kind of storytelling that we cannot fully see from our current vantage. After all, this is only the incunabula of social text. It was sixty years after Gutenberg built his printing press before anyone had the bright idea to number the pages. Who knows what social text innovations will be made in the decades to come?

Whether the advent of social reading and writing can replace the virtues of solitary reading and writing—their care and quiet empathy—with anything of equal merit remains to be seen. Maybe there will be a flowering of new prose styles. There was a burst of Greek lyric poetry in the seventh century when cheap papyrus suddenly became available. Couldn't our spree of social tech occasion another burst of creativity? There are smart people already at work exploring the possibilities. The poet Kenneth Goldsmith, for one, taught a course at the University of Pennsylvania called "Wasting Time on the Internet," in which digital distraction was mandatory because he wholeheartedly believes that the Internet's frenetic state can jumpstart new arenas for creative writing. A surrealist, "electronic collective unconscious" can produce new work, he says, "in ways that aren't yet recognized as literary."[152]

Great writers like Jennifer Egan have published stories in strings of hundreds of tweets (although, in a telling amalgam of new and old, Egan chose to publish hers using the *New Yorker*'s Twitter account). Alain de Botton wrote a book "live" at Heathrow Airport while passersby watched his illuminated screen (*A Week at the Airport* was both a stunt and a tour-de-force of writerly attention). And Margaret Atwood has published a zombie story on Wattpad (Atwood laughed off those who thought she should be "endorsing Literature, Capital L").[153]

Three days into my own attempt at social writing, I gave up. To allow the readers' likely responses to dictate the writing was exhausting, for one, and it was also anathema to the kind of storytelling I knew and loved. Where there had been purpose and singular personality, I was now attempting to cobble together a story that had no voice, no argument at all—an algorithmic narrative, designed to spit out plot points in reaction to any given input. I found this particular variant of social writing both frustrating and, ultimately, boring. "Morons," I muttered, snapping shut my laptop.

Perhaps future generations will hack the system, move at will between storytelling technologies. As for me, I was retreating from the social option. I began taking myself to the water's edge in order to read—away from the phone and the terrible Cyclops eye of my modem. On the seawall, bundled against wind and propped up with a sweater for a seat, I rediscovered a frame of mind that I was in danger of forgetting— real, trance-like reading that obliterated my anxieties, my fussing daily life. It was almost frightening—both the experience itself and the awareness that my reading style had strayed so far from the kind of reading I did as a child, when I became Holden Caulfield or Mary Lennox. When I found myself all alone and rehearsing another's life.

Long after my meeting with Oatley I realized what an unmitigated ass I'd been toward Anna Todd. Here I was, praising the merits of empathy, the bedazzled superhuman qualities that my old style of writing and reading supposedly afforded. And I had never given her social worldview a chance. Maybe that wall between readers and writers really must come down. In fact, why would it not? Those old stories, those novels we read, with their single plots and long-gone authors, are just as much a fabrication, a centuries-old fashion, a product of the fifteenth century's printing press. Don't we need new ways to tell our new stories about our new lives?

Each technology drops its own lens over your eyes. And who can say that the social media lens is any less viable than the printing press lens? Rarely are we granted something as beatific as a novel's resolution, anyway, whereas life does indeed splinter down several paths the way a Twitter feed might. Can any of us judge whether the age of printing or the age of screens best describes the way our lives wildly branch with each choice we make? Can we know which form of storytelling best captures the incalculable number of meanings in a single day?

After all, the fragile idea that your life is a cohesive story (that you will find your Heathcliff or survive a journey to Mordor), the idea you are a hero of *some* story, certainly isn't borne out by today's lived experience. Real life feels more like a Tumblr feed than a novel. Real life is random, overpowering, and scarcely knowable as it scrolls past our bewildered, blinking eyes. Anna Todd's work reflects twenty-first-century life in a way that work like my own may never do.

As for my social writing experiment, I sent the tech startup my botched attempt and told them to please waive the $100 fee they were offering. A week later I received an email back—an apology for taking so long to respond. They receive so many messages that mine had gotten lost.

10

Love Letters

A couple of dozen bright young men and women—all under thirty and all possessed of a pleased eagerness—are poised at their typewriters and wondering how to begin. Tea has been provided, and biscuits. Paper of different colours and designs has been distributed. All is pleasant; all is convivial. Still, a note of trepidation sounds here at the Regional Assembly of Text. The typewriters, lined up on both sides of a single enormous table, are classic models with names that portend great things—Underwood, Olympia, Remington, and Hermes. The hesitant clatter of keystrikes and the irrevocable *thunk* of carriage returns begin to fill the room. A woman with mounds of elaborate braids atop her head, perhaps twenty-two, brings her polished black nails to the keys, tries to produce an "I," falters.

Since 2005, a monthly letter-writing workshop has been offered here at the hipster-heavy end of Vancouver's east side. The space is normally a stationery store, but on select evenings it is transformed for the youths who attend. And many do. As the experience of typewriters and "real" letters grows more distant, a certain fetishization of those artifacts has emerged. As one participant told me, "Archaic things and future things are the same, as far as novelty goes. Getting to use old technology feels like getting to try tech from the future."

It is impossible not to compare their well-meaning fascination with the earnestness of the earliest letter writers, millennia ago, for whom a message on rough papyrus was the furthest thing from a lark. . . . A Roman soldier, out on the harsh frontier of Vindolanda by Hadrian's Wall, begs loved ones to send him a new pair of socks. A Greek statesman issues a violent set of instructions intended for a theatrical public recitation.[154] And then, today, Cleo sits at the Regional Assembly of Text and struggles to think of anything worth writing to her boyfriend.

"I didn't know there wouldn't be a delete button," frowns Alex. He is a thin young man in a faux-vintage Star Wars T-shirt, attempting to write a letter to his fiancée. He waves at the page in his typewriter, which is covered with misspellings and lines he has crossed out by hand. Alex is facing up to the fact that his initial thoughts are messier than he imagined. A sweet sentiment shines through the rubble all the same: "This is my first letter. My first real letter ever. Lucky, lucky you."

Not everyone is here to write love letters. One fellow tells me he's come "to type up some Oscar Wilde quotes because I figured typewriter font would look good." Others appear to be here more for the opportunity to post images on their

Instagram feeds; several smartphones are being used to capture chic impressions of "the authentic" in action.

A young woman tells me she's writing to her family, back in Copenhagen. "This is like spending an hour in my family's living room," she says. "I can be, I don't know . . . simpler. The slowness in the typing sort of makes me feel like I'm with them. I don't know."

When I retreat to the shop's counter to speak with co-founder Brandy Fedoruk, she tells me the letter-writing club has offered its young attendees a window into a near-extinct frame of mind. "On a phone or computer you can type faster than you can think," she says. "But a typewriter, it seems to me, matches the speed of thought."

Brandy's role during these events is that of the encouraging aunt. Attendees—who are used to writing to friends in a constant stream throughout the day—find themselves stumped when tasked with a larger, single report. They often don't know what to write or whom to write to. Many people here have never received a letter before.

One young woman, May, tells me that she's writing "to my boyfriend, to tell him we won't be texting anymore." I smile and say that sounds romantic—they may find they'll enjoy the anticipation of speaking face to face. But May frowns and bites her lip. "Oh, you don't understand. This is a breakup letter. When I say we won't be texting I mean we won't be in each other's lives."

I make my way toward the door as several more young people pile in. They're pointing at the typewriters as though they've spotted a pack of exotic creatures at a zoo. To them, the idea of writing from such a detached position, the idea of not receiving an immediate response, the idea of spending an hour on a single "message" is a kind of joke, an ironic posture.

And yet, for each of them, there's also a string of warm and hopeful thoughts:

I could finally tell her how I feel.

He would understand why I did it.

I might explain myself at last.

There was a Big Bang moment, after which the messages we sent each other would never be so removed and considered again. A moment when old ideas about sending precious morsels of text across expanses of space and time just shuddered, cracked in half, and exploded outward. The day was October 29, 1969. The time was 10:30 p.m. The place was a laboratory at UCLA run by Professor Leonard Kleinrock. His was one of four labs devoted to the creation of the ARPANET, the Internet's godfather. A forty-person team had been working in Kleinrock's lab, attempting to send a first message to colleagues at the Stanford Research Institute in Palo Alto.

Samuel Morse's telegraph was branded by the message "What hath God wrought?" but, 125 years later, Kline and his team had prepared no special utterance for the ARPANET—they were oblivious, in a way, to the profundity of the moment. There was no camera on hand, no proper recording at all of the online world's first missive. A handwritten log entry is all that marks the event, and it does so in dull pencil: "Talked to SRI host to host." They didn't even use an exclamation point.[155]

Charley Kline, a twenty-one-year-old student program-mer with boyish features and neatly parted hair, was working with Professor Kleinrock that night; it was he who sat down to tap out the message. With a banality that would later infuri-ate historians, Kline attempted to type the word "login." (The message, it was hoped, would allow Kleinrock's team to access a computer at the Stanford lab.) Kline was simultaneously on the phone with a programmer at Stanford called Bill Duvall and checked in as he went: "Did you get the 'l'? Yeah? Did you get the 'o'?" Then the system crashed before he could finish. But not before, a few hundred miles away, the poetic word "lo" glowed on a screen. The Internet (ARPANET, technically) had spoken its first word.

Did Bill Duvall (or any of the engineers over in Palo Alto) see those two illuminated letters as something profound? Was it an issuance from an oracle? *Lo and Behold.* Or even biblical? *Lo, the star, which they saw in the east . . .*

In an interview many years later, Kline admitted that it wasn't until the 1980s that he realized the significance of what he'd done that night—that his little "Lo" was like a first step on the moon.[156] Of course, "lo" hadn't been the intended word, but it's fitting, all the same, that the first online corre-spondence was a hail, a word used by orators to demand a crowd's attention.

———

In the decades since, that single "lo" has unfurled into the billions of messages we send each other every day. We have learned to deeply love the instantaneity and surety of contemporary messaging—we love it more, perhaps, than voice-to-voice communication. (One study of American smartphone users, ages eighteen to forty-four, found that, while 43 per cent said they "feel connected" when talking on the phone, 49 per cent feel connected when they send or received text messages.)[157] A removed and sanitized form of communication is the preference: while polled smartphone users spend an average of 132 minutes each day communicating on their devices, only 16 per cent of that time is spent on phone calls.[158] The rest is spent in a purely text-based realm—one that is safe and sure; one that can be obsessively edited. We have developed a system of micro love letters for the twenty-first century whereby we groom each other with the unending expectation of being groomed back—and groomed back *right now*.

Mobile tech makes micro love letters perpetual. Nowhere is this more obvious than in the reams and reams of messages issuing forth on dating sites—there, dick picks and "sup" texts are the valentines of the age. Marcus Frind, whose dating site PlentyOfFish manages the romantic interests of some sixty million users, told me that the move from desktop computers to mobile platforms has drastically increased the scale of messaging on sites like his. "You see three or four times as many messages being sent when people use the site on their phones," he told me. "They check their PlentyOfFish messages about ten times a day." Frind designed his site to be the safest and least offensive option (there are no "hookup" categories on PlentyOfFish, and certain triggering language will cause a user to be blocked). He wanted to turn the salacious implications of "online dating" into "just dating": as a result, his became the site people aren't embarrassed to use in public, on the bus or sitting in a café. Fully 85 per cent of the site's traffic now takes place on its users' phones.

I met, too, with OkCupid's co-founder Christian Rudder; his site manages around 7.5 million daily messages of love and lust. Rudder reports that, while message numbers go up, the average *length* of messages, predictably, plummets when users start interacting using their mobile app. Average message length on his site dropped from about four hundred characters in 2005 to around one hundred characters in 2014.[159]

Whether we cruise avatar galleries or not, that shift toward shallower and shallower messages is something we've all witnessed. The leisurely pace of handwritten letters is clipped down into billions of bundles of increasingly famished text. As a frenzy of erotic messaging becomes possible, complete sentences are reduced to grammarless suggestions, and then those burn away too, making way for emojis and photos. Rebecca Solnit, in her essay "We're Breaking Up," describes how this rush of brief messaging satisfies neither our need for connection nor our desire for disconnection:

> I think of that lost world, the way we lived before these new networking technologies, as having two poles: solitude and communion. The new chatter puts

us somewhere in between, assuaging fears of being alone without risking real connection. It is a shallow between two deeper zones, a safe spot between the dangers of contact with ourselves, with others.[160]

And so what passes for love letters inches, each year, into those shallows—the safe, yet unsatisfactory, middle ground.

Today, the app Yo allows only the single word "Yo" to be transmitted, its developers having ascertained that "poking" is often all that is desired. The after-sex selfie has become a meme, with satiated lovers sharing their post-coital bliss with followers. And one may monitor one's partner with an app like mCouple, which strives to "keep 'em honest" by giving each partner remote access to the other's phone. (The app gives you access to your partner's text messages and Facebook messages, along with a log of every call they've made. You can also track the exact location of your partner, thus ruling out an illicit rendezvous.).

These all have one thing in common: they secure affections and desires behind protective screens, even as they reduce them to issued cyphers. To me, all this is the opposite of the kind of faith that an old-fashioned love letter implies. The end result is a culture of Orwellian "comfort" where we refuse to wonder about another's desire, refuse to not know whether a second date will occur, refuse to trust that our boyfriends aren't visiting their old girlfriends at work. Such mysteries become intolerable anachronisms. Instead, we hover forever in the shallow middle that Solnit describes. A culture of "romantic" micro-messaging and compulsive surveillance emerges that's more in line with satiation than with longing, more interested in satisfaction than with the mysteries of sustained erotic yearning.

Perhaps fretting over these changes is a Luddite pursuit. But we ignore at our peril the fact that new technologies can have concrete effects on human sexuality. Here's a small example, from the work of Dutch sociologist Egbert de Vries. It seems that members of a particular African tribe had the custom of always lighting a new fire in their hut after sex. Normally, this required that someone go to a neighbouring hut in order to bring back a burning stick, thus making everyone's sex life a known quantity; the transparency promoted social cohesion (adultery was difficult). When matches were introduced to this tribe, all that went up in smoke. Suddenly sex could be entirely private and secretive.[161]

If something as simple as a box of matches can uproot the rituals and sexual habits of a culture, we shouldn't be surprised that other points of light—our billions of glowing phones, say—can do the same. As new communication technologies stake a claim to the old territory of love letters, they're stamping out a certain solitude that was once intrinsic to our love lives.

To be fair, the courtship mania that future lovers will enjoy is in some ways comparable to the inky handwritten love letters crafted by our ancestors. In their meagre way, they too were just capitalizing on the gizmos of the day. For example: after the advent of the printing press, paper production ramped up and the price of paper plummeted; there was a simultaneous rise in literacy (especially vernacular literacy, as opposed to Latin); and the concurrent creation of complex military, judiciary, and legal organizations necessitated reams of letters. Meanwhile, the dissemination of calligraphic manuals helped to standardize writing styles. In hindsight, all these factors conspired to create an explosion of written conversation where only isolated cases had survived before. As a culture of letter writing boomed, sparing a page or two for romantic sentiments suddenly became a possibility for everyday people. In 1635, King Charles I made the Royal Mail Service available to his subjects, with letters carried between posts by "postboys"—thus the word *postal*. Almost simultaneously, a profusion of popular books appeared, describing the best way to write letters—a new skill for a population eager to begin connecting with far-flung friends. This would have been a thrilling new power. The French diplomat Antoine de Courtin, writing in 1671, was nearly mystical when he referred to letter writing as the "dialogue of the absent."[162] These simple missives were a kind of magic, a form of long-distance social grooming that had never been available to the masses. By the eighteenth century the change was complete enough that English lovers began to send each other valentines—more than fifteen hundred years after Valentine was given a saint's day.

From a sixteenth-century milkmaid to a twenty-first century McDonald's employee, ordinary folk take advantage of whatever connective technologies are at their disposal. To a point, the same drives guide our behaviour across the centuries. When the stoic philosopher Seneca mocks people who rush to Roman ports and greet the arrival of mail-boats in the first century of the Common Era, the scene is not so different from a crowd at a twenty-first-century opera hall diving into their phones at intermission. The comparison only goes so far, however, before it strains credulity. Today's text messaging is not, in the end, just a speeded-up version of letter writing. The letters we did away with were qualitatively different.

Letters demand slower, more thoughtful work; they engage our entire hands and not just our fingertips; they make our confessions precious by withholding them in a silent interval between composition and delivery; and they locate our personal history among our own possessions, as opposed to a steel-lined server. The text message equivalent (though delightful) is no substitute for the drawn-out progression of true letters, the accumulation in the shoebox, the ruffled tops of hastily torn envelopes, the tactile history of the thing itself. And then, of course, there's the potential for destruction, for forgetting: old-fashioned letters can be tossed in the bonfire, whereas in the indelible world of email and smartphones, both parties have a copy. The ability to destroy evidence of love may be as important as the ability to preserve it.

These are just a few of the hard-to-quantify qualities that transcend the more basic "information retrieval" that contemporary messaging technologies are so good at. Qualities like these result in an aura of specialness around hard-copy letters. I'm using Walter Benjamin's concept of "aura" here— aura being the ineffable quality that disappears when something "can be reproduced by technological means."[163] It's because of that cumulative aura that old letters are often seen as the surest expression of a person's character. Even one of the earliest commentaries on letters—from a little-known Athenian called Demetrius—notes that "everyone writes a letter in the virtual image of his own soul."[164] No one has said as much about Snapchat.

A letter is an act of faith—the solitary letter writer, working for hours, perhaps, at a single expression from one human heart to another, must assume a connection to someone who is absent and non-responsive for maybe weeks at a time. As the critic Vivian Gornick has it: "To write a letter is to be alone with my thoughts in the conjured presence of another person. I keep myself imaginative company. I occupy the empty room. I alone infuse the silence."[165] One presses beyond the happenstance of spoken speech (and the casual reassurances of texting and email) into an ordered expression of things that requires removal from chatter. And yet that conjured person does sit by our side. When we take the time to write long letters to those we care about, we uncover a part of them that was not revealed before, not at dinner parties, nor cafés, nor even lying together in rumpled sheets.

Which is what makes the love letter such an ideal tool for the pursuit of solitude's third gift. It isn't just a way to express oneself; it is a way to understand each other. From Pliny's letters to his wife in the first century of the Common Era, to Beethoven's "immortal beloved" letters, to James Joyce's frankly pornographic missives to Nora Barnacle, the history of love letters always includes an appreciation for the *lack* of communion, the delaying of desire. And in that empty space the writer has a chance to puzzle through the complexities of the human heart.

As the twenty-first century lurches forward, though, we find that love letters—so awkward, so slow, so exhausting to compose—are an endangered species. We forget that romantic connections benefit from solitude nearly as much as the beloved's company.

To understand what's gone missing, I decided to look way back in time—to the twelfth century—to a love, and a stack of letters, that survived against all odds.

One fateful night, in the year 1118, as the handsome French theologian Pierre Abelard lay asleep in his bedchamber, a group of strange men bribed their way into his home and assembled around his bed. The man who had sent them, the Canon Fulbert, was well known to Abelard. Fulbert was the uncle of Heloise, the girl whom Abelard had been tutoring. The girl whom Abelard had impregnated. The girl whom Abelard had removed to a convent of nuns, in the town of

Argenteuil. Fulbert was outraged by the insult to his family, and that night he took his bloody revenge. The men seized Abelard by his arms and legs. As Abelard screamed, they sawed off his testicles.

It was a tidy matter of honour. Abelard later wrote to a friend, "They cut off the parts of my body whereby I had committed the wrong of which they complained."[166]

The child—a boy named Astrolabe, after an Islamic astronomical instrument—was left with Heloise's sister and largely disappeared from history's records. Instead it's their letters that have echoes through history, the letters Abelard and Heloise wrote to each other long after their love could never be consummated again. Heloise became a nun and Abelard became a monk. Separated in convents and monasteries, they remained connected through their writing.

Abelard's epistolary affection does not match Heloise's. He writes to insist that she repent of their sins: "Offer a perpetual sacrifice of prayers to the Lord for our many great aberrations." But a wimple cannot stifle Heloise's desires. She writes back:

> In my case, the pleasures of lovers which we shared have been too sweet—they cannot displease me, and can scarcely shift from my memory. . . . Even during the celebration of Mass, when our prayers should be purer, lewd visions of those pleasures take such a hold upon my unhappy soul that my thoughts are on their wantonness instead of on prayers.[167]

Abelard is sometimes criticized for his relative coolness. But we should look at his situation with a practical eye: his testicles have been removed. We know that such a profound severance results in the collapse of a man's sexual drive. And we should not underestimate the effect of humiliation.

What was felt before the castration? We can only guess. A bundle of long-lost love letters, believed by some to be the notes these two wrote before their romance met its tragic end, may give us a glimpse. From a testosterone-equipped Abelard: "You are buried inside my breast for eternity. . . . You keep me company right until I fall asleep; while I sleep you never leave me, and after I wake I see you, as soon as I open my eyes, even before the light of day itself."[168] On another occasion, the same lover writes:

> How fertile with delight is your breast, how you shine with untouched beauty, body so full of moisture, indescribable scent of yours! Reveal what is hidden, uncover what you keep concealed, let that whole fountain of your most abundant sweetness bubble forth.[169]

Whatever passion Abelard once felt for Heloise, it burned off and was replaced by a studious care in the end.

The true lesson about love letters, here, comes from Heloise—and her alone. Across the distances of space and time, she begs Abelard for a reconnection. "While I am denied your presence," she writes, "give me at least through your words—of which you have enough and to spare—some sweet

semblance of yourself."[170] Letters are the way she preserves
that "sweet semblance" of a love that has been taken from her.
The vagaries of fate have removed her beloved, but in letters,
in their luxury of contemplation, she attempts an understanding between them. Her letters are long and winding; they are
maps of her despair and also her desire; they sing of an affection that does not end when the beloved is removed. When
Alexander Pope wrote his heroic epistle about the two, more
than five centuries after Heloise's death, he declared:

> Heav'n first taught letters for some wretch's aid,
> Some banish'd lover, or some captive maid;
> They live, they speak, they breathe what love
>   inspires,
> Warm from the soul, and faithful to its fires.[171]

Pope admires how letters can "speed the soft intercourse
from soul to soul / And waft a sigh from Indus to the Pole."[172]
Perhaps this is what fascinates readers of Heloise's letters: the
miracle of connection (with a past lover, with a present lover,
with the past self, with the present self) in the midst of a determined solitude.

History is rife with Heloises. Only the cynical say such
people pine after a lost cause. The removed person may indeed
never return (and some things, as Abelard knew better than
anyone, can't be undone). But in the solitary composition of
our love letters we heal wounds and bridge distances. When
we write them we experience communion *within* our solitude.

They inspire the sensation Byron describes as "the feeling infinite, so felt / In solitude, where we are least alone."[173] They make the paradox of Eros obvious—showing us that we desire best that which we cannot have.

11

The Failing Body

Death

Death is, of course, the final and inviolate solitude.

The obliteration it promises we view with horror, if we look on it at all. It is a final separation so unthinkable—literally unthinkable—that most of us manage to live our entire lives without wholly contemplating it. Indeed, as Freud pointed out, we can never truly comprehend our own death since, when we try to imagine it, we remain spectators instead—like Huckleberry Finn attending his own funeral. For this reason, Freud writes, "in the unconscious every one of us is convinced of his immortality."[174] We know *of* death but don't plan on becoming acquainted.

And yet, despite this horror and incomprehension, we of course owe death everything.

Things have been dying for about as long as they've been living. Here on Earth, that accounts for four and a half billion years. Generation after generation lives, reproduces, and expires. Each generation passes on the best of itself to those that follow. But the process of evolution—which carried us from base elements to primordial goop to you—works only so long as previous generations die off. For this reason, we, like all animals, have a senescence program built into our genes that ensures our aging and collapse after we pass our prime reproductive years. (This involves the progressive shortening of telomeres, the genetic "bumper" system that protects the start and end of each chromosome. As cells divide, this fraying eventually triggers DNA damage.) In the simplest of terms: the very metabolism that keeps us alive has side effects that accumulate and eventually produce pathology and death. It turns out that Samuel Beckett was more on the ball than he knew when he wrote, "Birth was the death of him." Life, indeed, kills us.

Everything we have accomplished—all our art and poetry and science—is the direct product of these deaths, since it's all the product of evolution. And so the International Space Station spins 249 miles over your head thanks to death; the Star Wars franchise is worth $30 billion thanks to death; our Hadron Collider and reality TV and United Nations and strawberry sorbet and *Paradise Lost* and Cristiano Ronaldo's legs, and on and on and on, all exist thanks to the trillions of deaths that carried us forward. Far from being senseless or horrible, death is the fuel that runs this planet-sized engine.

A world without the final solitude of death would be a disaster. And yet the immortal state, denial of Darwinian progress, is exactly the state we clamour toward. I began this chapter by calling death an inviolate solitude, one there is no getting around. But plenty are now working to prove me wrong.

Our foraging ancestors managed a life expectancy of only thirty or forty years. Infant mortality was the major stumbling block, and it remained incredibly common until quite recently. For example, right up until the twentieth century, death claimed a quarter to a third of children in agricultural societies. Smallpox, measles, and diphtheria made the business of growing up a deadly game of odds. But eventually things looked up—and quickly. In 1960, an American's life expectancy at birth was seventy, and it rose to seventy-nine by 2014; in Afghanistan it rose from thirty-two to sixty during that span of years.[175] These numbers are of course markedly unfair, and yet—across the globe—they are still rising.

Meanwhile, genetic engineers have managed to double or treble the life expectancy of the *Caenorhabditis elegans* worm by modifying its genes.[176] It is presumed that—whether by arresting our senescence programs or by flooding our bloodstreams with janitorial nanobots that can clean up the cellular mess—medical breakthroughs will eventually lead to even further, perhaps enormous, advances in our life expectancies, carrying us far past the presumed barrier of 120 years.[177] Such life-extending advances would fit neatly into an emergent belief that death is unnatural and something we ought to conquer—or at least cover up.

As scientific advances extend our lives, they also seem to

hack away our interest in (and respect for) the central role that death plays. We sweep it, tuck it, hide it away. I am thirty-six years old and I have never seen a dead person. Modernity itself encourages new, less death-centric approaches to life. "Beginning in the eighteenth century," Yuval Noah Harari points out,

> ideologies such as liberalism, socialism, and feminism lost all interest in the afterlife. What, exactly, happens to a Communist after he or she dies? What happens to a capitalist? What happens to a feminist? It is pointless to look for the answer in the writings of Marx, Adam Smith, or Simone de Beauvoir.[178]

A big part of the project of modernity has been to focus on the quantifiable reality that surrounds us. But modernity has also had its casualties, and an acquaintance with death is one of them. And so death's insistence on an everlasting solitude, an everlasting separation from the world we live in, has become something to either "cure" or ignore.

This fuzzy dream of ours, the dream where we conquer death, played out for centuries in the work of our science fiction writers. But those fantasies have been replaced by bona fide efforts today. And it is perhaps no surprise that the quest for immortality is being led by the eternally optimistic denizens of Silicon Valley. In 2013, for example, Google announced the formation of Calico (the California Life Company), which means to hack the biology that determines our aging. Then, in 2014, the Palo Alto Longevity Prize was launched; it offers $1 million to those who can "hack the code of life" and "solve aging." Cambridge researcher Aubrey de Grey, a member of the prize's advisory board, summed up their philosophy nicely when he called aging a "medical problem" as opposed to a natural process. Since we are machines, goes the thinking, aging and age-related death must be flaws in our hardware or programming, flaws we should be able to fix. What's more, de Grey believes that denying future generations an indefinite lifespan is "immoral."[179] The technology historian Patrick McCray has called this desire to hack death an ideological one for Silicon Valley, where "disruptive technologies" can inspire a religious fervour. As McCray told the *Guardian,* "If you have made your billions in an industrial sector that is based on precise careful control of zeroes and ones, why not imagine you could extend this to the control of atoms and molecules?"[180]

De Grey could have a point, though. Don't we have a moral imperative to make life as healthy as possible? To minimize suffering? Then again, more than one moral imperative can sway us at the same time; and they can sway us in different directions. Isn't it also immoral to set future generations up for perpetual economic failure? And what else would we call a situation where young adults compete for jobs and resources with their great-great-grandparents? Folk in my own generation already complain bitterly about baby boomers who refuse to retire. It is difficult to imagine any cohort calmly handing over the reins to industry and governance and real estate because people two hundred years younger think it's their turn.

An even worse scenario would be the possibility that our great-great-grandparents do *not* remain competitive and instead descend into dementia en masse. Longer lifespans have not, thus far, saved us from such ravages. Roughly 36 million people were living with dementia in 2012, and the World Health Organization predicts that number will double by 2030 (to 65.7 million) and triple by 2050 (to 115.4 million).[181] For a number of reasons, physical immortality may simply be untenable. We can buck against it all we like, but entropy has a stubbornness. I'm reminded of Leonid Andreyev's short story depicting the afterlife of Lazarus: he escapes his own death only to become a rotting zombie full of "sinister oddities" without the peace of a proper end. His face is blemished by a "deep and cadaverous blueness," his lips are swollen and bursting, his body is puffed with gaseous waste. Lazarus weeps bitterly and tears his hair. His family and friends forsake him, so changed is he; he's shunned like a leper.

Ultimately, carbon-based life may be too frail for immortality. And so our urge to escape the Final Farewell pushes us toward the ultimate in technological solutionism: we dream of doing away with our awkward bodies altogether. Who needs these corruptible bags of bone and blood? We could instead live in the cloud. . . .

In the picturesque town of Iași, in northeastern Romania, the tech entrepreneur Marius Ursache—handsome and confident—sits in his glass-walled office and tells me about death.

"There are, of course, three deaths we each experience. There is the moment you lose control of yourself, there is the moment the body actually passes away, and there is the last time anyone speaks your name."

It is this third death, the moment we disappear from human memory, that Ursache's startup Eterni.me is tackling. For about $10 a month, the service will collect your personal data in order to build an avatar that can stand in for you after your demise. This avatar will know everything about you worth knowing, and your friends/admirers/ancestors will be able to grill it for details. It will look like you, too, and will converse with users so they may feel connected—if not exactly to you then to the embodiment of your digital slime. ("We decided to bring the avatar to life, despite the *creepiness* criticism.") In a sense, what Eterni.me offers is a Skype from the beyond.

"Every day, for one to three minutes," Ursache tells me, "the avatar will ask you questions about yourself." The avatar's questions are well directed because it has full access to your social media; it might, for example, ask how you feel about that new friend you made on Facebook. The avatar will also ask for big-picture information. What are your first memories? How did you feel about your father? "The avatar will replace diaries," says Ursache, with a quiet smile. "It's going to transform what it means to be human because you'll become more reflective during your life."

The site is partly inspired by science fiction: Ursache is a fan of Isaac Asimov's Foundation series and Philip K. Dick's

Ubik. He's also into films about artificial intelligence like *Her*—in which a man falls in love with his operating system—and avatar-run platforms such as *Second Life*, where millions of users design an online world for their avatars to enjoy. What all these pop references share is an expectation of the digital beyond—a place where human experience is expanded and protected by a technological foster system. But Ursache has more personal motives, too. As his grandmother died of Alzheimer's, he saw how the disease stripped her of memories. This seemed intolerable to a man who had spent his life building clean solutions to life's messiness. His grandmother's loves, her beliefs, her travels and readings and jokes—all stripped and lost, forever. If only there were a way to safeguard the treasure trove of her mind.

As we spoke, in the spring of 2016, Ursache's compact staff of five worked nearby; a dog cruised the hallway; it seemed like any other ambitious little startup. The team was busily prepping for their public launch. What had begun as a thought experiment at MIT's Entrepreneurship Development Program was about to become a reality. Thirty thousand people had signed up for Eterni.me's services, and it didn't even exist yet. Hundreds more were writing in every day. Ursache had tapped into something real.

Eterni.me has joined the ranks of an expanding e-death industry that includes Deathswitch (which, if you like, will release your passwords and take-to-the-grave secrets after you are, in fact, taken to a grave) and If I Die (which allows you to record a farewell message that will be posted, post-mortem, to your Facebook wall). Social media's soft insistence on perma-connectivity thus makes a Ouija board of the Internet, one that provides nearly mystical relationships with spirits. How fantastic, to enjoy such a communion with the dead!

Of course, real memories of people, as experienced by survivors, are nothing like the so-called memories dished out by computers. Computers cannot remember at all; they can only recall. It's strange this distinction isn't made more often. Real memories divide, mutate, live. Scientists now agree with Jorge Luis Borges, who said, "Every time we remember something, after the first time, we're not remembering the event, but the first memory of the event. Then the experience of the second memory and so on." Through a brain process called reconsolidation, every retrieval of a given memory actually changes it. As one expert, Nelson Cowan, told me: "We edit the past in light of what we know now. But we remain utterly unaware that we've changed it." Our memories of lost loved ones, then, are morphing things—not static files. The promise of something like Eterni.me is that we can circumvent our minds' failings to bridge the separation death imposes. But to circumvent in that way is to miss the point of mourning and human memory. The Talmudic maxim claims, "We don't see things as they are; we see things as *we* are." And I think we can similarly say, "We don't remember people as they were; we remember them as *we* are." To deny the fallible, shifting approach with which we remember the dead is to deny the fallible, shifting nature of our relationships.

Then again, even if future mourners pass up the digital Lazarus on offer, the dying themselves may find it impossible to give up on a tech company's promise of eternal connection. As global birth rates plummet, I imagine we'll count less on the old idea of "living through our children" and more on a new idea of "living through our avatars." The futurist and computer scientist Ray Kurzweil has been arguing for years that we'll soon be able to merge our minds into computers. By 2029, he tells us, computers will boast emotional lives as convincing as any human's. By 2030, we'll be flooding the body with millions of nanobots that will rebuild immune systems, essentially wiping out disease and allowing us to add more than a year of life expectancy for each year of real time (thus, Kurzweil himself intends to stay ahead of the game and never die at all). By 2050, these fleets of nanobots will grow so numerous and skilful they'll be able to assemble an entire bionic body for the human mind to inhabit.[182] One that neither rots nor rusts.

It was noticed early on that computers improve at a nearly exponential rate while we humans dodder along, barely improving ourselves at all. Such growth, it is imagined, almost necessitates a "singularity"—a moment in the near future when our technology becomes so advanced that it either propels us or drags us to a higher state of being. Kurzweil's ideas do sound like science fiction, but he is hardly a crank—he has been feted with numerous honours, including the National Medal of Technology and a position at Google as their director of engineering. Silicon Valley has always nurtured those who trade in the fantastic.

Kurzweil is joined by many less qualified futurists who share his dream. In 2016, a "transhumanist philosopher" called Zoltan Istvan argued that artificial intelligence should replace the American president (along with other world leaders) since the AI would be less "selfish." (To be sure, this is one advantage of not having a self.) Then, once artificial intelligence reaches a certain threshold, human beings, says Istvan, will be invited into its intelligence.

> We will be merged, basically directly. I see it in terms of: The world will take 100 of its best scientists— maybe even some preachers, religious people, some politicians, people from all different walks of society—and everybody will plug-in and mind upload at one time into this machine.[183]

The guest list to end all guest lists. These euphoric visions amount to something that one friend of mine termed "a silicon rapture."[184] Like the Christian rapture, this one promises to shuttle a select group up into an eternal and happy holding pen. And this imagined end point for the biological body would be the final triumph over death's solitude, a final exit from the clunky, carbon-based contraptions we've been saddled with by Darwinian evolution. Good riddance. All "evolution" cares about is the perpetuation of genes, little amino acids all in a row; the singularity promises that individuals, whole minds, can live on—we save souls instead of code.

The singularity theory can be traced back to the rumina-
tions of the prodigal mathematician John von Neumann. His
vision was described this way in the Bulletin of the American
Mathematical Society: "The ever-accelerating progress of
technology . . . gives the appearance of approaching some
essential singularity in the history of the race beyond which
human affairs, as we know them, could not continue."[185] Since
then, the idea of computers operating at a thousand, a million,
a billion times the capacity of a human brain has been one of
the animating forces of both science fiction and the vanguard
of the tech industry. It's a dream that's gaining shape. In
Silicon Valley there is even a well-respected Singularity
University, founded in 2008.

Naturally, a serious conundrum pops up before we get
too far down this road. Any effort to produce these digital,
immortal selves relies on the assumption that we are compu-
tational entities in the first place, that the self can be reduced
to that which our machines may process.

As John Searle pointed out (back in chapter 6), it is no
stretch to imagine that machines can harbour life and consciousness (we are, after all, a kind of machine ourselves), but
to suggest that life and consciousness can be prolonged via the
perfect recall of a mere computer of data, a number-cruncher
flickering its ones and zeroes, is another matter. Still, the
emergent e-death industry (including Eterni.me and the
other harbingers of the singularity) seeks to save a portion of
our humanity by preserving our data in the silicon forever.
Believers in the singularity suggest that *all* of humanity will

later live on in the cloud. It's in this way that death—the grand solitude that made us what we are—is slaughtered.

The Body's Kind Betrayal

In the end, our belief in the singularity, the silicon rapture, or even just the e-death industry signals a rejection of the lonely limits built into our frail, mortal bodies. Year by year, we spend more time projecting ourselves beyond our bodies with avatars and social media. And still we're trapped by the narrow facts of bodily life; this proper number of calories in, this tiny wedge of atmospheric comfort between freezing and broiling. The brutal limits of the flesh.

Some solitudes cannot be outrun. And yet it's so often in the failings of our solitary bodies that we come to know our humanity. It can seem absurd, at times, to admit that we are bound inside envelopes of water and genetic hand-me-downs. But the fact of our mortal bodies can also be the thing that shakes us awake.

I was first paralyzed at sixteen. I'd been dreaming my usual dream, in which a shadow-man shoots me in the back of the head, and I woke at the usual spot—as the black heat spread across my crown. But this time I did not scramble up from the pillow. I could not. It took a moment to realize that I'd failed to sit up, and another moment to discover my eyes would not open, either. Nothing moved at all but my heart and lungs, and

208

now they were nervously thrumming like caught animals. For two swollen minutes I commanded my body to move, then began conceding little parts of me—could I at least move my head? No. My arms? No. Could I turn my palm or raise a finger? And, with each failure, a panic crawled across my body. The panic, in turn, brought a message, something that's whispered only to the paralyzed: *You* are only a spark inside this four-limbed apparatus. You are alone in the cave of your mind. The "I" of you is just a story in a robot's head.

Everyone's brain takes care to paralyze its robot at night; otherwise our bodies would act out our dreams—we'd run from imagined monsters, howling and naked, into the street. This temporary paralysis saves our bodies from ourselves. And, for a small percentage of people, the little limbic switch managed by our two amygdala, that hormonal alarm that snaps the body back to life each morning, can go rusty. We wake to find ourselves trapped in a warm-dead body. This rust seems to first accumulate in the teenage years, perhaps brought on by the advent of anxiety, or the discovery of alcohol. Or perhaps it's just a symptom of the brain's laziness, a shrugging disavowal of our failing bodies.

That morning, when I first woke paralyzed, I did not wonder why, any more than a fox in a leghold trap wonders why. I only raged against the hold. In my little bed, within my little body, I was hurling myself away from metal teeth, 'til at last the switch gave way and I was expelled back into the world. I arrived voice-first, gulping with choky, can't-breathe cries that woke my mother down the hall. She appeared, silhouetted in the doorway, her sleepy face a mixture of worry and complaint, arms crossed over a cotton sleep shirt. She squinted as I tried to describe it: "Like I was dead, or frozen, or going crazy. . . ."

"That's weird," she said as I sputtered to a stop. There was nothing to be done, though; biting her lip, she flicked off the hall light and padded back to her own dark room. I sat on that bed a long time, propped up and knocking my head against the wall whenever sleep tugged me down. I waited hours for the first permissive touches of daylight.

On some unacknowledged level I may have expected this collapse, or at least I wasn't wholly surprised. The idea that the flesh will betray us is no news to a sixteen-year-old boy. Even my pores were indecent, either turning inward with cystic acne or spinning out wiry leg hairs long before the other boys became hairy.

My limbs were out of order, too: Osgood-Schlatter disease made the bones, ligaments, and muscles in my legs grow at different speeds, pricking out tears of pain whenever I climbed or descended stairs. It felt as though my true legs had been skinned and crammed into a smaller metal set. The disease meant I had to watch from grassy sidelines while my PE class swooped around the field like flocking birds. Mr. Pearson did not believe in doctor's notes and considered my ailment a personality issue. It was true, at any rate, that I was glad to be free of those games—I could not throw or catch, much less understand the screaming instructions of abler boys. I sat in overgrown weeds, patiently breaking twigs into smaller and smaller pieces, and looking up to watch the boys crash into each other on the field. I remained set apart—pretentious and unwilling. And lonely. Loneliness seemed to be what my body meant.

It was another decade before I learned to stop myself from using the bawling cure for my monthly bouts of sleep paralysis; eventually I learned to come out of it more quietly. It coincided with meeting Kenny. That first week we slept together, he sat cross-legged on the bed and reported, "It's like a dog growl." In fact, the growl has become my antidote: if I growl enough, it will wake my limbs; if I manage to produce something that rings in the external world, it will bring me back to life. I need signals from beyond my body, something outside myself. The dog growl works, or else Kenny, seeing my clenched distress, can shake me out of limbo.

The panicky trap is always escaped after a few minutes. But I see, in those moments, the concrete limits of my body and how very lonely I am always in danger of becoming. I see the limits of my brain—this hive of eighty-six billion neurons, terribly complex yet still incapable of merging with anything outside itself. And this book is perhaps proof I've become obsessed by the limits of this confederacy of cells.

I stood one night in our apartment, pressing my hands on the walls and going on about an article I'd read that said nothing ever touches anything else. The electrons orbiting each atom keep us hovering away from things at an unfathomably small distance. I pushed on the wall and focused on the minute pores in the paint; someone had done a hasty job during the last renovation and you could see a haze of blond underneath the white. I said, "So not even now, not anything."

Kenny laughed and said, "Did you just realize that?"

Later, I'm asleep beside Kenny and he's begun to shudder; it's so violent it wakes me. Kenny suffers from sleep paralysis, too. We've each learned to recognize the difference between a bad dream and our disorder. I shake him back to life.

Kenny pushes himself up on his elbows, stares forward into the half-light, and then over at me. Wordless, he burrows into his pillow, flops onto his back; he's searching for a position that will keep him safe from the trap. I settle down and move my hand in circles on his chest to be sure of him.

This is the trauma we keep seeing in each other. It makes a long, sparse pattern across our days so that we stumble, move on, stumble, through the year. But it's always almost there: the shaking, the growling, the haunted coffin of a single body. Then this violent wrenching back to the larger world; the startled intake of breath. And, finally, the fact of someone else's body; this nearly connecting company in the dark.

Just a final example . . .

One day my grandmother told my mother, "I don't feel right. Something is wrong." In the emergency room she was asked to locate the discomfort and she waved her hand with an incantatory gesture over half her body.

She hoped to be in and out of hospital in a few days; she was not. Her bowel had twisted and her oxygen levels were

dangerously low. Several links in her spinal column had crumbled, compressing her back into a human-sized question mark.
After surgery for the twisted bowel, her time in the hospital led
to pneumonia and decreased kidney function—either one of
which is often fatal for the elderly. Meanwhile, shoals of blood
clots had collected in her lungs, threatening to suffocate her.

Months passed in the hospital. My grandmother became
confused, paranoid, and disoriented. And bit by bit it came to
pass that her body was no longer her own. She couldn't even
swallow but was hydrated by one of the thirteen tubes the
nurses had threaded into her. She lay there, immobile, disgraced
by sponge baths and fed so many drugs she lost her mind.

"Get me out of here!" she rasped to any family member
who came to visit. "I need you to help me escape!" The doctors, the nurses, the room were all trying to kill her. "Why
won't you help me?" she wept. "Bring David in here. Bring
Suzanne. Bring Noel. They'll get me out."

Meanwhile, beyond the room's narrow window, a few
sparrows had become trapped behind some wire netting. Or
so she kept insisting. Perhaps they were only nesting there; I
don't know. My grandmother fretted over the birds obsessively. "They're trapped! Go and help them!"

At three one morning the phone rang at my parents'
home. "You'd better come in. This may be it." And the family
convened. The aunts who weep wept, and the other aunts who
prefer to gather coffee orders did their dogged rounds. And
yet my grandmother remained lodged in her failing body.
There were several conferences with doctors, who didn't

believe she'd survive, but, slightly bewildered, they were then proven wrong.

Four months after her arrival my grandmother was released. She now lives with a rotation of caretakers who are summoned with a bell when it is time to rise from bed. Her body shudders awake each morning, pushes off the faded sheets.

I visit her at home and when she hugs me hello it is bold and lasts longer than our WASPy roots would normally dictate. I take a recorder, determined to capture her childhood stories. I could play them to my children one day, I tell myself. But I can't look her in the eyes and ask for permission; it would mean giving something away, somehow. When we say goodbye she holds me tighter still. It shocks me how tight.

In my grandmother's embrace, and in the way Kenny shakes me awake from paralysis (or I shake him), I see that the body's solitude forces us to reach out. After all, it is the inevitable fact of our body's isolation, its hard limits—along with the fact of our death—that makes us love one another so well in the brief, bewildering chance that we have.

12

The Cabin in the Woods

By the time I finish this tuna sandwich, I'll have been alone—completely alone—for longer than I've ever been before.

It's a startling thought. But, sitting here on this rotting deck, and looking out over both the ocean and the last thirty-six years, I find it's true. Weirdly true. I have never, in my life, been completely alone for longer than twenty-four hours. Always, there was some quiet interaction with the guy making my Americano, at least. Or, if I was stuck in my apartment with the flu, there'd be an email exchange while curled in the nest of my duvet. But there was always some connection, some comfort.

From infancy onward, I have been perpetually witnessed, judged, hugged, chatted-up. . . .

But that changes now. I've taken the ferry from Vancouver to Pender Island, about two hours off the coast of British Columbia. From the docks, I hiked another two hours to my family's cabin. An old A-frame, built by my grandparents in the days when a parcel of land on an island's waterfront wasn't so impossible a thing to purchase. There's a rope swing from when I was five; it dangles noose-like from one of the trees. A set of rotten steps leads me, muddy and skidding, down to the pebble beach where my brothers and I used to build rafts out of driftwood. We tied logs together with ropes of bull kelp.

The cabin door shunts open and there's the smell of cedar planks, wet dog, ashes. I tug provisions from my pack: one week's worth of oatmeal, raisins, tuna fish, canned chili. A paper bag of apples, one for each day.

I've come here for a week with myself. I plan on not just doubling or tripling my solitude record but stretching it to the point where I'm talking to myself. Before I left the city, friends and families shrugged at the project—what's a week?—until I asked them how long *they'd* ever been on their own.

"Without people, without a phone, without Internet?"

"Right. On your own."

"What about Facebook?"

"That's actually on the Internet."

"Right."

"Yeah."

"Um . . ." After puzzled internal calculations, most people arrived at the same number I had: twenty-four hours. At some point, due to flu or crippling depression, they had spent one full day without human connections. Younger friends had a harder time; most couldn't remember a time when they were cut off from all society for more than twelve hours. (And remember, they got eight free hours just for falling asleep.)

As for myself, I felt vaguely resentful when I noticed that twenty-four hours was as long as I'd gone. I was naive, maybe even unmanly, for having been so coddled. Psychologically obese. There was a sense that I needed to stop contemplating things and just buckle down, alter my solitude diet. And then I came across an idea from the pianist Glenn Gould, an eccentric genius who abruptly stopped giving concerts in 1964; he had retreated into the solitude of the studio and told an interviewer, "I've always had a sort of intuition that for every hour you spend with other human beings you need X number of hours alone. Now, what that X represents I don't really know; it might be two and seven-eighths or seven and two-eighths, but it's a substantial ratio."[186]

A ratio! A needful number of hours alone for every hour spent in the crowd. It's such a sensible proposition. But I realized I never experimented with this ratio in a significant way. Had never figured out what balance of solitude and company I loved best. I'd mostly been making do with however much solitude life threw at me, never insisting on an alternative to society the way a vegetarian might insist on an alternative to steak. And so I resolved to start with an extreme and figure out my Gouldian solitude ratio from there.

So. Here I am. A cabin in the woods, a creaking A-frame. Between the road and me there are ninety silent acres of forest. And seven long days.

On my first night I'm beset by child-like fears. The antique fridge makes a sporadic knocking sound, precisely the sound an axe murderer would produce, were he to taunt his victim from the other side of a rain-slicked window. The cedar beams creak in a chilling sequence, as though designed to imitate footsteps in the dark. There is something utterly impossible about the night if one is not used to it. We so seldom acknowledge it, bleaching it out with streetlights and music and television. So much so that, when confronted with its true weight, its pillow-on-face smothering, there's a panicky urge to flee. But I haven't given myself that option. Flee where? Into the black woods? Instead, I peer out the window, watching washes of dusk get inked over in darkening layers, as though a painter's wet brush is being drawn, inch by inch, down each cedar branch. And I try to take Robert Frost's advice to become "acquainted with the night." I sit by the window, in wool socks and flannel pyjamas, a cup of hot water at my lips, and tell myself why I'm here: I'm here to become acquainted with the night.

A rustle outside, something shakes a branch by leaping— where? And then silence again as the wild progresses with its infinite work, oblivious to the skittish human in his wooden box. It is painfully obvious that the night has no particular wish to become acquainted with *me*.

Lunchtime on day two, I finish my tuna sandwich and realize I've now been alone longer than ever before.

The first changes are obvious. My ability to self-regulate is in crisis, for example. I'm in danger of devolving into a pre-verbal cave-person. The sort of creature who eats all the snacks instead of sticking to the carefully planned Ziploc portions.

To instill a sense of order, I force myself to make the bed. This works remarkably well. I immediately want to shower and have tea after that. Patterns reassert themselves.

But that doesn't mean my mental processes aren't tweaking themselves. Twenty-four hours in, I am unabashedly holding conversations with myself. It remains unclear whether this is a sign of a declining or ascending mind. Meanwhile, there's this persistent awareness of my own frailty. It occurs to me that if I slip on a seaweed-slimed rock down on the beach and break my neck, or drink poisoned water, or just suffer a run-of-the-mill stroke, it will be a week before my body is missed at all. By the time they find me (he was so brave, in his solitude!), the hawks and sea otters will have eaten the best bits.

It's not as hard to stick it out when I remember the newness of what I'm trying to give myself. When I become freaked out by the silence or—more often—grow deadly bored, I remember that this was never going to be easy, that withdrawal symptoms are to be expected.

Thoreau believed that we're all artists in the end, and our bodies, our lives, are the material we work with. The decision to spend our hours this way or that should be as considered as the strike of a sculptor's chisel. That's a lot of pressure. This boredom, these terrible nights by the fireside, these cotton-quiet hours—there's an expectation I'll find some remedy here. By my second day, nothing has come. But more little scraps from Thoreau egg me on:

A voice said to him—Why do you stay here and live this mean moiling life, when a glorious existence is possible for you? . . . All that he could think of was to practice some new austerity, to let his mind descend into his body and redeem it.[187]

By the end of day two not a single magical voice has visited me. My mind has descended into my body and gotten lost. I miss everyone. I miss my bed and my television and Kenny and dear old Google. I stare hopelessly for an hour at the ocean, a coruscating kind of liquid metal; I feel the urge to change the channel every ten minutes. But the same water goes on and on, like a decree. Torture.

By day four at the cabin I have, out of necessity, changed my attitude. One cannot stare at the ocean for a week, waiting for epiphanies. Watched pots, and all that. So I look around, narrow my eyes. Around this time it occurs to me that Thoreau wasn't the only guy who liked living in a solitary cabin. Ted Kaczynski, the Unabomber, lived alone in the woods, too. There is a right way and a wrong way to go about this.

I go on enormous hikes through the woods. I begin to notice things I never noticed in all the years I've been coming here with carloads of other people. There are boulders of massive granite strewn everywhere, which do not match the shale and sandstone the island is made of—these boulders, with their toupees of stringy moss, look like catapult ammo from a skirmish in heaven. They are rude and magnificent and utterly out of place. It must have been a receding glacier that left them, twenty thousand years ago. The larger trees, and only the larger trees, have charred black marks on the first four metres of their trunks, signs of a massive forest fire that must have taken place a century ago. Time deepens, deepens terribly, so that I suffer vertigo to look into the green-and-black tangle.

At one point I meet a doe on a path, and we stare at each other for a curious moment. Her absurdly alert ears align with inky Bambi eyes to form two exclamation points on her word-less face. I raise a hand in greeting and think perhaps we're experiencing a mystical recognition, but then the doe sticks her tongue out at me—actually sticks it out—and springs away. I watch her cotton flash of a rear disappear into the brush and I stand there like nature's biggest loser.

The author and aviator Anne Morrow Lindbergh used to go to a seaside cabin, too. She writes in *Gift from the Sea* about this shifting of perspectives, the strange way that such retreats produce a richness of experience. The benefit begins with discomfort as we leave our crowded lives:

> Parting is inevitably painful . . . like an amputation. . . .
> It is as if in parting one did actually lose an arm. And
> then, like the star-fish, one grows it anew; one is whole
> again, complete and round—more whole, even, than
> before, when the other people had pieces of one.[188]

The arms grow back. Different colours sometimes. And one has the intimation that the eventual return to society will be just as damaging; I will tear off some portion of what I grew here.

Near the end of this lonely week my thoughts stop floating so much and return to the problem of solitude in a digital culture. Only now, out on the meditative trail I've been hiking before and after my crackers-and-apple lunch, I'm thinking about it differently, more expansively. Things here call for wide lenses.

From this dirt vantage, all that clicking and sharing and liking and posting looks like a pile of iron shackles. We are the ones creating the content, yet we're never compensated with anything but the tremulous, fast-evaporating pleasures that social grooming delivers. Validation and self-expression, we are told, are far greater prizes than the measly cash that flows upward to platform owners. This, as the media critic and film-maker Astra Taylor has pointed out, is digital feudalism. She writes that "sites like Facebook and Tumblr offer up land for content providers to work while platform owners expropriate value with impunity."[189] We are the unwashed mob in this scenario. Meanwhile, the platform systems we live by can expropriate no value from solitude, and so they abhor it.

I do not mean that Mark Zuckerberg over at Facebook and Susan Wojcicki over at YouTube are actively plotting against the forces of solitude from within their marble palaces. I mean, rather, that the Zuckerbergs and Wojcickis of the world (whatever their genius and wealth) have been co-opted by forces still larger than themselves, forces that only raise up anything and anyone that inspires connectivity.

It has been suggested by the memeticist Susan Blackmore that our technologies grow and change by the same principles that govern biological evolution. Given the fundamentals of variation, selection, and heredity, one *must* have evolution—and it is therefore by evolution's law, and not the "genius" of any CEO, that our technologies advance, becoming more viral and enmeshed with each succeeding generation. The cognitive biologist W. Tecumseh Fitch, using a related metaphor, has argued that we've all become metaphoric neurons in a global brain, synthesizing into a single, homogenous intelligence. "We . . . are on the brink of a wholly new system of societal organization, one spanning the globe with the metaphoric axons of the Internet linking us together."[190] This transformation parallels biological evolution toward complex bodies: though our ancestors were just free-floating cells for three billion years, they eventually gave way to multicellular cooperatives until they could only *survive* as a collective. A sweat gland cell or cortical hair shaft cell now cannot thrive without joining the alliance of thirty-seven trillion cells whose teamwork amounts to one *self*.[191] Likewise, the Internet makes its dendritic progression across the globe, sending off new shoots in all directions until individual humans coalesce to form a super-body that cannot disassemble itself.[192]

H. G. Wells anticipated this enormous sweep toward anti-solitude when he wrote *World Brain* in 1938, a work not of sci-fi but of social criticism in which he argues for the creation of "a widespread world intelligence conscious of itself"[193] that would undo the singular dictators who had ruled us until then. The vision is sometimes utopic, sometimes terrible—this coalesced, planet-sized consciousness that need never be severed from its own enormous company.

Step. Step. On the trail, where I am literally retracing my own footprints in the crusting mud, all these expansive notions seem bizarre, like scenes from a prescient science fiction movie. And it's somehow obscene to think: if I brought a phone out on this trail, the spiralling tendrils of the Internet would be here, too; indeed, they *are* here already, waiting for something to hook onto. What's different about this dirt-trail contemplation is that I can now see the weirdness of it all. None of it looks inevitable from here as I kick at a rotting trunk, scour the sky for eagles.

The path is getting too close to the road now. As I turn back toward the cabin, I try to imagine another, slower-growing Internet—one that requires two-way links, so that any online connection would have to be approved by both parties. Maybe it would be more curated, less ramshackle. It would allow for the creation of cathedrals, too, instead of only bazaars. But it would also encourage class warfare, I suddenly realize, with "undesirables" being ignored and isolated, unlinked. As my imaginary scenario plays out, I see a two-way-link Internet where the rich and educated enjoy a playground of "higher" conversation, leaving the poor behind to labour in the data mines of the first string of platform technologies. The thought is chilling.

Is there no middle road, a way to secure some isolation within the glory of all that connectivity? Is there not a way to get past Lindbergh's starfish problem, where essential parts of our selves are ripped off each time we enter and exit our solitude? Is there a third way that each person, alone, could discover for themselves?

On my last evening, I read a collection of Barbara Gowdy stories and drag my plastic chair around the rotting deck to catch the last of the light. Eventually this sun-hunting takes me off the deck entirely; I'm sitting in the tall dead grasses off to one side. The wasps buzz drunkenly around and, to my astonishment, I can hear a dog barking on the next island over. There's an eight-hundred-metre stretch of salt water between us. My mind reels at this effect—it's like an axe on a trunk. These flying vibrations.

As the last of the sunlight begins to shutter I realize I'm sitting beneath the arbutus tree where my grandfather's ashes were scattered. I never knew him. There is a photo of him holding me when I was a newborn, though—I'm reaching up and trying to chew his nose.

I've grown so used to talking to myself these past days that talking to a dead grandparent feels sociable by comparison. As the night comes on, I jam my hands in my armpits for warmth and tell him some things about my life so far. And I am a child again, a very small child. And being alone in that dusk does feel a little like being dead, too. The solitary and the dead know the same trick, anyway—they both know how to be unaccountable.

I wake to rain on my final day. It is mid-October now, and during this week away I've witnessed the crunching turn of autumn. The routine clicks on automatically: make the bed; make the oatmeal; make the coffee; stare at the wet-gem colours of sunrise on ocean.

Mornings are the best chance we get, every day, to recall our solitude. They are brief glimpses into a default mindset that arises before the world pours too much noise into our eyes and ears. Most of my peers now reach for their phones the moment they awaken—their solitary morning moments are only brief flashes of void that they instinctively extinguish. But something happens when we stretch out that brief flash, live inside it longer.

Long ago, in the mornings, I'd lie abed indulging in private reveries; in recent years there's been, instead, a desire to hop online and tally everything I missed while unconscious. The week in the woods has repaired that part of me, though. This sunrise on breeze-shivered water is not something to run from.

Thoreau says, "Mornings bring back the heroic ages." He writes about a first tiny piece of sonic input at breakfast: the buzz of a mosquito. And the mosquito's hum is, to him, a Homeric requiem. "An Iliad and Odyssey in the air, singing its own wrath and wanderings."[194] Thoreau felt this way not because the mosquito's hum was any louder than usual but because he had cultivated in his mornings a state of solitude in which encounters became rare, and therefore precious.

When a blind child is given sight by a surgeon, the child must be introduced to light and colour and objects in a creeping fashion so as not to terrify her. The bandages are removed in a darkened room, and it's not uncommon for the child to grow upset and disoriented on first experiencing the "gift" of sight. In a smaller but similar way, the return to company after the experience of being alone requires an inching-in, too.

As I trudge in the rain back along sloshy trails, I move through drooping cedar forest, past rock shelves wrapped in sparkling moss and meadows of sword ferns. Then I see power lines and then a paved road. I walk along the asphalt for a while and come upon some farmhouses. Inside one a child is practising the piano—a stilted "Twinkle, Twinkle, Little Star" weaves through the rain's drumming. A man in a truck comes down the road and as he approaches he raises two fingers from the steering wheel in greeting. I smile and then worry that I somehow botched the encounter. Could he see through the windshield that I had smiled? Should I have waved?

The ferry is crowded, too crowded. I collect some lunch from the cafeteria and wince at the grating shouts of the staff and customers—talking, talking, talking. But, minutes later, as I purchase a magazine in the gift shop, I start chatting up the woman at the till—to an embarrassing degree. I am so starved for conversation that the weather, for the first time in

227

my life, becomes a truly worthwhile topic. Finally she says, "Sorry, there are other people," pointing to the line that's formed behind me. Walking away with my rolled-up *Esquire*, I think of how many elderly people I've dismissed as they went on about rain and sun.

I find a quieter corner of the ferry and hunker down, watch the whitecaps. I drink vending-machine coffee. I think to myself, I did not die. There is no rotting body on Pender Island.

As we adapt to evolving technological environments, as we respond to shifts in living arrangements, as we inhale the rhetoric and poetics of our own time, our relationship to solitude keeps changing.

What we're beginning to notice, from the midst of this tech-gorged moment, is that solitude is a resource we can either nurture or allow to be depleted. Think of a forest. For centuries we could walk among dense stands of firs when we chose, or profit from cutting the same trees down without much care as to whether nature at large would be materially damaged. Then a line was crossed and we found ourselves starved for green space.

Today, thanks to platform technologies, profit is wrought as much by the dismantling of mental resources as it is by the dismantling of natural resources. We have learned to harvest the solitude of others. Profiteers produce social grooming technologies, and agents of distraction swarm around us. Solitude is consumed and depleted as surely as Brazilian rainforests are toppled and the tar sands of Alberta are sucked dry. This is how we make an Easter Island of the mind.

When I finally get home, with a week of beard and rain-heavy clothes, Kenny is surprised to see me. "I didn't know exactly when you were coming back," he says, hugging me hello. From my puddle in the entranceway I can see little changes that have taken place in my absence. There's a new potted vine on top of the bookshelf; Kenny started a Michael Chabon novel; there's a stack of mail on my desk.

"I missed you," I say. And saying it, I realize it's the first time I've properly missed someone in years. In a rush I think, *I'm going to marry this man.* This was the biggest bonus of all— the fact that working to find myself meant gaining others, too.

"How was it?"

His innocent question is like a blow, though, because now I have to explain myself. After such a long stretch of self-containment, with my mind fashioning its own unchecked meaning, the duty of communication feels like a deep puzzle. I haven't thought up a way to describe my solitude yet, to make it sensible to others. I drop my pack to the floor. A little helplessly, I smile over at him and try to sketch the borders of a place we can only ever know on our own.

Notes

1. R. I. M. Dunbar, "The Social Brain: Mind, Language, and Society in Evolutionary Perspective," *Annual Review of Anthropology* 32 (2003): 163–81.

2. R. I. M. Dunbar, "Coevolution of Neocortex Size, Group Size and Language in Humans," *Behavioral and Brain Sciences* 16 (1993): 681–735.

3. The World Bank, "Internet Users (per 100 People)," http://data.worldbank.org/indicator/IT.NET.USER.P2/countries?display=graph.

4. Roselyn J. Lee-Won, Leo Herzog, and Park Sung Gwan, "Hooked on Facebook: The Role of Social Anxiety and Need for Social Assurance in Problematic Use of Facebook," *Cyberpsychology, Behavior, and Social Networking* 18, no. 10 (2015): 567–74.

5. Pew Research Center, *Social Media Update 2013*, January 2014, http://www.pewinternet.org/files/2013/12/PIP_Social-Networking-2013.pdf.

6. ABI Research, "More Than 30 Billion Devices Will Wirelessly Connect to the Internet of Everything in 2020," May 9, 2013, https://www.abiresearch.com/press/more-than-30-billion-devices-will-wirelessly-conne.

7. John Tagliabue, "Swiss Cows Send Texts to Announce They're In Heat," *New York Times*, Oct. 1, 2012, http://www.nytimes.com/2012/10/02/world/europe/device-sends-message-to-swiss-farmer-when-cow-is-in-heat.html.

8. Natalie Angier, "Edward O. Wilson's New Take on Human Nature," *Smithsonian Magazine*, April 2012.

9. "Always Connected for Facebook," IDC Research Report, https://www.idc.com/prodserv/custom_solutions/download/case_studies/PLAN-BB_Always_Connected_for_Facebook.pdf.

10. Katy Steinmetz, "No, You Can't Auction Off Public Parking Spaces in San Francisco," *Time*, June 23, 2014.

11. Micha Kaufman, "Five Reasons Half of You Will be Freelancers in 2020," *Forbes*, Feb. 28, 2014.

12. MIT, "Live Singapore," http://senseable.mit.edu/livesingapore.

13. Ester Buchholz, *The Call of Solitude* (New York: Simon & Schuster, 1997), 16, 17.

14. Martin Miller, "Unattached, thank you, and loving it," *Los Angeles Times*, September 2, 2004.

15. Henry David Thoreau, *Walden* (1854; repr., New York: Knopf, 1992), 121.

16. Stephanie Cacioppo et al., "Loneliness: Clinical Import and Interventions," *Perspectives on Psychological Science* 10, no. 2(2015): 238–49.

17. Miller McPherson, Lynn Smith-Lovin, and Matthew E. Brashears, "Social Isolation in America," *American Sociological Review* 71, no. 3 (2006): 353–75.

18. Robert Putnam, *Bowling Alone* (New York: Simon & Schuster, 2001), 2.

19. Ross Douthat, "All The Lonely People," *New York Times*, May 18, 2013, http://www.nytimes.com/2013/05/19/opinion/sunday/douthat-loneliness-and-suicide.html.

20. A. R. Teo et al., "Does Mode of Contact with Different Types of Social Relationships Predict Depression in Older Adults?" *Journal of the American Geriatrics Society* 63, no. 10 (2015): 2014–22.

Notes

21. Anthony Storr, *Solitude* (1988; repr., New York: Free Press, 2005), 34.
22. Anne O'Hare McCormick, "Radio's Audience: Huge, Unprecedented," *New York Times*, April 3, 1932.
23. Storr, *Solitude*, 146.
24. Christopher R. Long and James R. Averill, "Solitude: An Exploration of the Benefits of Being Alone," *Journal for the Theory of Social Behaviour* 33, no. 1 (2003), 21–44.
25. Storr, *Solitude*, 147.
26. Storr, *Solitude*, 34–35.
27. Long and Averill, "Solitude," 24.
28. Reed Larson, M. Csikszentmihalyi, and R. Graef, "Time Alone in Daily Experience: Loneliness or Renewal?" in *Loneliness: A Sourcebook of Current Theory, Research, and Therapy*, ed. L. A. Peplau and D. Perlman (New York: Wiley, 1982), 40–53.
29. "Louis C.K. Hates Cellphones," *TeamCoco*, September 20, 2013, http://teamcoco.com/video/louis-ck-springsteen-cell-phone.
30. Robert Kolker, "Attention Must Be Paid," *New York Times*, Sept. 25, 2014, http://www.nytimes.com/2014/09/28/books/review/a-deadly-wandering-by-matt-richtel.html.
31. Carl Jung, *Collected Works*, vol. 7 (Princeton: Princeton University Press, 1967), paragraph 757.
32. Jung, *Collected Works*, vol. 6, paragraph 267.
33. Jung, *Collected Works*, vol. 7, paragraph 266.
34. Philip Koch, *Solitude: A Philosophical Encounter* (Chicago: Open Court, 1994), 57.
35. Donald Winnicott, "The Capacity to Be Alone," *International Journal of Psychoanalysis* 39 (1958): 416–20.
36. Donald Winnicott, "Primary Maternal Preoccupation," in D. W. Winnicott *Collected Papers: Through Paediatrics to Psychoanalysis*. London: Tavistock, 1958.
37. Thoreau, *Walden*, 120–21.
38. Timothy D. Wilson et al., "Just Think: The Challenges of the Disengaged Mind," *Science* 345, no. 6192 (2014), 75–77, http://www.sciencemag.org/content/345/6192/75.

39. James Boswell, *The Life of Samuel Johnson*, vol. 3 (Boston: W. Andrews and L. Blake, 1807), 115.

40. Mary Helen Immordino-Yang, Joanna A. Christodoulou, and Vanessa Singh, "Rest Is Not Idleness: Implications of the Brain's Default Mode for Human Development and Education," *Perspectives on Psychological Science* 7, no. 4 (2012): 352–64.

41. Kieran C. R. Fox et al., "The Wandering Brain: Meta-analysis of Functional Neuroimaging Studies of Mind-Wandering and Related Spontaneous Thought Processes," *NeuroImage* 111 (2015): 611–21.

42. Bob Samples, *The Metaphoric Mind: A Celebration of Creative Consciousness* (Boston: Addison-Wesley, 1976), 26.

43. Felicity Mellor, "The Power of Silence," *Physics World* 27 (2014): 30.

44. Ibid.

45. Anthony Storr, *Solitude* (1998; repr., New York: Free Press, 2005), 198.

46. Alison Gopnik, "Explanation as Orgasm and the Drive for Causal Understanding," in *Cognition and Explanation*, ed. F. Keil and R. Wilson (Cambridge, MA: MIT Press, 2000), 299–323.

47. Sigmund Freud, "Creative Writers and Day-Dreaming," *Standard Edition of the Complete Psychological Works of Sigmund Freud*, vol. 9, trans. James Strachey (London: Hogarth, 1959), 146.

48. Virginia Woolf, "A Room of One's Own," in *The Norton Anthology of English Literature*, vol. 2, (New York: Norton, 1983), 1983–4.

49. Anthony Storr, *Solitude* (New York: Free Press, 2005), 198.

50. Rainer Maria Rilke, *Letters to a Young Poet*, trans. Stephen Mitchell (New York: Vintage, 1986), 41.

51. Franz Kafka, *Letters to Felice*, ed. Erich Heller and Jürgen Born, trans. James Stern and Elisabeth Duckworth (New York: Schocken Books, 1973) 155–56.

52. Bertrand Russell, "In Praise of Idleness," *Harper's Magazine* (Oct. 1932).

53. Sebastian de Grazia, *Of Time, Work and Leisure* (New York: Vintage, 1994), 341.

54. Dean Takahashi, "Candy Crush Saga Maker Reports Strong Q1 with $569M in Adjusted Revenue and 61 Cents-a-Share Profit," *VentureBeat*, May 14, 2015, http://venturebeat.com/2015/05/14/candy-crush-saga-maker-king-beats-wall-streets-expectations; Eli Hodapp, "Candy Crush Made More Money Than All Nintendo Games Combined Last Year," *Toucharcade*, May 30, 2014, http://toucharcade.com/2014/05/30/candy-crush-made-more-money-than-nintendo; Chris Morris, "Why Activision Spent $5.0 Billion on 'Candy Crush' Creator King Digital," *Fortune*, Nov. 3, 2015.

55. Interview with the author, May 12, 2015.

56. Aldous Huxley, foreword to *Brave New World*, 2nd ed. (New York: Bantam Books, 1953), xxviii.

57. Clive Thompson, *Smarter Than You Think* (New York: The Penguin Press, 2013), 11, 18.

58. Vannevar Bush, "As We May Think," *Atlantic Monthly*, July 1945.

59. Dante Gabriel Rossetti, "The Day-Dream," in *Collected Poetry and Prose*, ed. Jerome McGann (New Haven: Yale University Press, 2003), 194.

60. Quentin Crisp, *The Naked Civil Servant* (New York: Penguin Books, 1997), 61.

61. Penny Arcade, "Quentin Crisp and Penny Arcade in Vienna," YouTube video, March 13, 2012, https://www.youtube.com/watch?v=NTttQs-UhgA.

62. Quentin Crisp, *The Naked Civil Servant*, x.

63. Ibid.

64. Quentin Crisp, *Doing It with Style* (London: Eyre Methuen, 1981), 50.

65. Ibid., 119

66. Ibid., 127

67. Ibid., 145

68. Richard Alleyne, "English Language Has Doubled in Size in the Last Century," *Telegraph*, Dec. 10, 2010.

69. Mike Isaac, "For Mobile Messaging, GIFS Prove to Be Worth at Least a Thousand Words," *New York Times*, Aug. 3, 2015.

70. Neil Postman, *The Disappearance of Childhood* (New York: Vintage Books, 1994), 70.

71. Tom Standage, *Writing on the Wall* (New York: Bloomsbury, 2013), 182.

72. Janet Echelman, "Skies Painted with Unnumbered Sparks," http://www.echelman.com/project/skies-painted-with-unnumbered-sparks.

73. Alexander Mordvintsev, Christopher Olah, and Mike Tyka, "Inceptionism: Google Deeper into Neural Networks," *Google Research Blog*, June 17, 2015, http://googleresearch.blogspot.ca/2015/06/inceptionism-going-deeper-into-neural.html.

74. Doris Lessing, *Prisons We Choose to Live Inside* (Toronto: House of Anansi, 1991), 49.

75. John Snell, *The Nazi Revolution* (Boston: D. C. Heath, 1959), 7.

76. Quentin Crisp, *The Naked Civil Servant*, 142.

77. Rian Keating, "Quentin Crisp Interviewed by Rian Keating, May 1983," YouTube video, Jan. 27, 2015, https://www.youtube.com/watch?v=WBPwWrFWHAc.

78. J. McCarthy, "Ascribing Mental Qualities to Machines," in M. Ringle (Ed.), *Philosophical Perspectives in Artificial Intelligence*, ed. M. Ringle (Atlantic Highlands, NJ: Humanities Press, 1979), 161–95.

79. John Searle, *Minds, Brains, and Science* (Cambridge, MA: Harvard University Press, 1984), 30.

80. "Nielsen: Global Consumers' Trust in 'Earned' Advertising Grows in Importance," *Nielsen*, April 10, 2012, http://www.nielsen.com/ca/en/press-room/2012/nielsen-global-consumers-trust-in-earned-advertising-grows.html.

81. James Gleick, *The Information* (New York: Pantheon Books, 2011), 406.

82. Barry Schwartz, "The Paradox of Choice," TED video, July 2005, http://www.ted.com/talks/barry_schwartz_on_the_paradox_of_choice?language=en.

83. "Data Never Sleeps," *Domo*, April 2014, https://web-assets. domo.com/blog/wp-content/uploads/2014/04/ DataNeverSleeps_2.0_v2.jpg.

84. Solomon E. Asch, "Effects of Group Pressure Upon the Modification and Distortion of Judgments," in *Groups, Leadership and Men*, ed. Harold Guetzkow (Pittsburgh: Carnegie Press, 1951), 177–90.

85. Neil Postman, *Technopoly* (New York: Vintage Books, 1993), 196.

86. Matthew Crawford, *The World Beyond Your Head* (New York: Allen Lane, 2015), 19.

87. James Surowiecki, *The Wisdom of Crowds* (New York; Anchor Books, 2005), 31.

88. Lewis Carroll, *Sylvie and Bruno Concluded* (London and New York: Macmillan, 1893), 169.

89. Marshall McLuhan, *The Gutenberg Galaxy* (Toronto: University of Toronto Press, 2010), 174–76.

90. M. Viswanathan, "Discover Deliciousness with "Explore" in Google Maps," *Google Maps*, Sept. 2, 2015, http://google-latlong.blogspot.ca/2015/09/discover-deliciousness-with-explore-in.html.

91. Jerry Brotton, "Let's Take Maps Back From Google," *Telegraph*, June 1, 2013, http://www.telegraph.co.uk/culture/10091089/ Jerry-Brotton-lets-take-maps-back-from-Google.html.

92. Uri Friedman, "12 Maps That Changed the World," (*The Atlantic*, Dec. 30, 2013), http://www.theatlantic.com/international/ archive/2013/12/12-maps-that-changed-the-world/282666.

93. Carroll, *Sylvie and Bruno Concluded*, 169.

94. Caitlin Garlow, of FleishmanHillard, email message to author, Sept. 22, 2015.

95. James Gleick, *Faster* (New York: Vintage Books, 2000), 93.

96. "Google CEO Eric Schmidt on Privacy," YouTube video, Dec. 8, 2009, https://www.youtube.com/watch?v=A6e7wfDHzew.

97. Dave Eggers, *The Circle* (New York: Knopf, 2013), 129–130.

98. Neil Postman, *Amusing Ourselves to Death* (New York: Penguin, 1985), 60.

99. Mark Twain, *Historical Romances* (New York: Library of America, 1994), 126.

100. Richard Byrd, *Alone: The Classic Polar Adventure* (Washington, DC: Island Press, 2003), 84–85.

101. Ibid., 7, 6.

102. Ibid., 213–15.

103. Richard Byrd, *Alone* (London: Neville Spearman, 1958), 206.

104. Stephen Moss, *Natural Childhood* (National Trust, 2012), http://pooleprojects.net/National%20Trust_Natural%20Childhood%20Brochure.pdf.

105. Richard Louv, *Last Child in the Woods: Saving Our Children from Nature-Deficit Disorder* (Chapel Hill, NC: Algonquin Books of Chapel Hill, 2005), 34.

106. Yuval Noah Harari, *Sapiens: A Brief History of Humankind* (Toronto: McClelland & Stewart, 2014), 79.

107. Margaret Visser, *Much Depends on Dinner* (Toronto: McClelland & Stewart, 1987), 156.

108. Kathleen McAuliffe, "If Modern Humans Are So Smart, Why Are Our Brains Shrinking?" *Discover* (Sept. 2010), http://discovermagazine.com/2010/sep/25-modern-humans-smart-why-brain-shrinking.

109. Harari, *Sapiens: A Brief History of Humankind*, 83.

110. World Health Organization, "Urban Population Growth," Global Health Observatory data, http://www.who.int/gho/urban_health/situation_trends/urban_population_growth_text/en.

111. Plato, *Phaedrus*, in *Plato: Complete Works*, ed. John M. Cooper (Indianapolis: Hackett Publishing, 1997), 510.

112. William Wordsworth, "The Tables Turned," *The Norton Anthology of English Literature*, vol. 2 (New York: Norton, 1993), 135.

113. Richard Louv, *The Nature Principle* (Chapel Hill, NC: Algonquin Books of Chapel Hill, 2012), 20.

114. Serge Caparos et al., "Do Local Perceptual Biases Tell Us Anything About Local And Global Selective Attention?" *Psychological Science* 24, no. 2 (2013), 206–12.

115. Duncan Jeffries, "Is Technology and the Internet Reducing Pupils' Attention Spans?" *Guardian*, March 11, 2013, http://www.theguardian.com/teacher-network/teacher-blog/2013/mar/11/technology-internet-pupil-attention-teaching.

116. Sean Coughlan, "City Living 'Makes It Harder to Concentrate,'" BBC News, Feb. 20, 2013, http://www.bbc.com/news/education-21506132.

117. Gregory N. Bratman et al., "Nature Experience Reduces Rumination and Subgenual Prefrontal Cortex Activation," *Proceedings of the National Academy of Sciences of the United States of America* 112, no. 28 (2015): 8567–72.

118. Robert S. Ulrich et al., "Stress Recovery During Exposure to Natural and Urban Environments," *Journal of Environmental Psychology* 11, no. 3 (1991): 201–30.

119. Bum Jin Park et al., "The Physiological Effects of *Shinrin-yoku* (Taking In the Forest Atmosphere or Forest Bathing): Evidence from Field Experiments in 24 Forests Across Japan," *Environmental Health and Preventive Medicine* 15, no. 1 (2010): 18–26; Qing Li et al., "Forest Bathing Enhances Human Natural Killer Activity and Expression of Anti-Cancer Proteins," *International Journal of Immunopathology and Pharmacology* 20 (2007): 3–8.

120. Rebecca A. Clay "Green Is Good for You," *American Psychological Association* 32, no. 4 (2001): 40, http://apa.org/monitor/apr01/greengood.aspx.

121. Susan S. Lang, "A Room with a View Helps Rural Children Deal with Life's Stresses, Cornell Researchers Report," *Cornell Chronicle*, April 24, 2003, http://www.news.cornell.edu/stories/2003/04/room-view-helps-rural-children-deal-stress.

122. Eva Selhub and Alan C. Logan, *Your Brain on Nature* (Toronto: Wiley, 2012).

123. Laura Smith, "Rx: 50 mg Nature, Ad Lib," *Slate*, July 25, 2014, http://www.slate.com/articles/health_and_science/medical_examiner/2014/07/doctors_prescribing_outdoors_time_nature_is_good_for_you.html.

124. Nathan Donato-Weinstein, "Google Campus Plan Would Explode the Concept of Buildings, Workspace," *Silicon Valley Business Journal*, Feb. 27, 2015.

125. Eugene Kim, "Amazon Is Building Three Giant Glass Domes Filled with Endangered Species at Its New HQ," *Business Insider*, June 29, 2016, http://www.businessinsider.com/amazons-giant-glass-domes-are-filled-with-endangered-species-2016-6.

126. Matthew Crawford, *The World Beyond Your Head* (New York: Allen Lane, 2015), 94.

127. Ibid., 27.

128. Jane Austen, *Pride and Prejudice* (1813; New York: Signet Classic, 1980), 30.

129. Ibid., 154.

130. William Hazlitt, *Hazlitt: Selected Essays,* ed. George Sampson (Cambridge: Cambridge University Press, 1958), 143.

131. Wendell Berry, *What Are People For?* (Berkeley, CA: Counterpoint, 2010), 11.

132. Marcel Proust, "On Reading Ruskin," ed. and trans. Jean Autret, William Burford, and Philip J. Wolfe (New Haven: Yale University Press, 1987), 113.

133. Virginia Woolf to Ethel Smyth, July 29, 1934, *The Letters of Virginia Woolf*, vol. 5, ed. Nigel Nicolson and Joanne Trautmann (New York: Harcourt Brace Jovanovich), 319.

134. In August 2014, Mar gave a lecture titled "Fiction and Its Relation to Real-World Empathy, Cognition, and Behavior," at the American Psychological Association's 122nd Annual Convention.

135. Natalie Jarvey, "Victorious Launches App for Fan Fiction Author Anna Todd," *Hollywood Reporter*, Feb. 25, 2016.

136. Kathryn Zickuhr and Lee Rainie, "E-reading Rises as Device Ownership Jumps" (Washington, DC: Pew Research Center, Jan. 16, 2014).

137. Dartmouth College, "Digital Media May Be Changing How You Think: New Study Finds Users Focus on Concrete Details Rather Than the Big Picture," *ScienceDaily*, May 8, 2016, http://www.sciencedaily.com/releases/2016/05/160508151944.htm.

138. Jennifer Maloney, "The Rise of Phone Reading," *Wall Street Journal*, Aug. 14, 2015.

139. Kevin Kelly, "Scan This Book!" *New York Times Magazine*, May 14, 2006.

140. Clay Shirky, "Why Abundance Is Good: A Reply to Nick Carr" *Encyclopaedia Britannica Blog*, July 17, 2008, http://www. britannica.com/blogs/2008/07/why-abundance-is-good-a-reply-to-nick-carr.

141. Maryanne Wolf, *Proust and the Squid* (New York: Harper Perennial, 2007), 47.

142. John Brockman, ed., *Is the Internet Changing the Way You Think?* (New York: Harper Perennial, 2011), 271.

143. Maryanne Wolf, *Proust and the Squid* (New York: Harper Perennial, 2007), 168.

144. Susan Greenfield, *Mind Change* (New York: Random House, 2015), 13.

145. Marshall McLuhan, *The Gutenberg Galaxy* (Toronto: University of Toronto Press, 2011), 54.

146. Neil Postman, *The Disappearance of Childhood* (New York: Vintage Books, 1994), 12.

147. Alberto Manguel, *A History of Reading* (Toronto: Vintage Canada, 1998), 42.

148. Dan Kois, "How One Direction Super Fan Anna Tod Went From Waffle House Waitress To Next-Big-Author With Erotic Fanfic Series 'After,'" *Billboard,* July 17, 2015, http://www. billboard.com/articles/magazine/6634431/anna-todd-after-one-direction-fan-fiction-book-deal-movie-rights-profile.

149. Bob Stein, "Original Invite Letter," *Sidebar,* Institute for the Future of the Book, http://www.futureofthebook.org/sidebar/invite.html.

150. Jakob Nielsen, "How Users Read on the Web," Nielsen Norman Group, Oct. 1, 1997, http://www.nngroup.com/articles/how-users-read-on-the-web.

151. Jakob Nielsen, "E-Mail Newsletters: Increasing Usability," Nielsen Norman Group, Nov. 29, 2010, http://www.nngroup.com/articles/e-mail-newsletters-usability.

152. Kenneth Goldsmith, "Why I Am Teaching a Course Called 'Wasting Time on the Internet,'" *New Yorker*, Nov. 13, 2014, http://www.newyorker.com/books/page-turner/wasting-time-on-the-internet.

153. "The Happy Zombie Sunrise Home" has done well, with 1.2 million reads at time of writing.

154. Simon Garfield, *To the Letter* (New York: Gotham, 2014), 36, 47–49.

155. "The First Internet Connection, with UCLA's Leonard Kleinrock," YouTube video, Jan. 13, 2009, https://www.youtube.com/watch?v=vuiBTJZfeo8.

156. AOL Mail Team, "A Chat With Internet Pioneer Charley Kline," AOL Mail Blog (Oct. 28, 2011), http://mailblog.aol.com/2011/10/28/a-conversation-with-internetpioneer-charley-kline.

157. IDC Custom Solutions, "Always Connected for Facebook," IDC Research Report, March 27, 2013, https://www.idc.com/prodserv/custom_solutions/download/case_studies/PLAN-BB_Always_Connected_for_Facebook.pdf.

158. Ibid.

159. Christian Rudder, *Dataclysm* (New York: Crown Publishers, 2014), 65.

160. Rebecca Solnit, *The Encyclopedia of Trouble and Spaciousness* (San Antonio, TX: Trinity University Press, 2015), 258.

161. Neil Postman, *Technopoly* (New York: Vintage Books, 1993), 27.

162. Antoine de Courtin, *The Rules of Civility; or Certain Ways of Deportment Observed in France, Amongst All Persons of Quality Upon Several Occasions* (London: J. Martyn and John Starkey, 1703), 169.

163. Walter Benjamin, *The Work of Art in the Age of Mechanical Reproduction* (New York: Penguin Books, 2008), 7.

164. Garfield, *To the Letter*, 98.

165. Vivian Gornick, *Approaching Eye Level* (Boston: Beacon Press, 1996), 162.

166. Peter Abelard and Heloise, *The Letters of Abelard and Heloise*, trans. Betty Radice (London: Penguin Books, 1974), 17.

167. Ibid., 68.

168. Ibid., 239.

169. Ibid., 243.

170. Ibid., 53.

171. Alexander Pope, "Eloisa to Abelard," *Works* (London: W. Bowyer for Bernard Linot, 1717), E-10 884, E-10 885, E-10 3938, E-10 3947, Fisher Rare Book Library (Toronto).

172. Ibid., 2256.

173. Lord Byron, "Childe Harold's Pilgrimage," in *The Norton Anthology of English Literature*, vol. 3 (New York: Norton, 1993), 490.

174. Sigmund Freud, *Reflections on War and Death*, trans. A. A. Brill and Alfred B. Kuttner (New York: Moffat, Yard & Co., 1918), Bartleby.com, 2010, http://www.bartleby.com/282/2.html.

175. World Bank, "Life Expectancy at birth, total (years)," http://data.worldbank.org/indicator/SP.DYN.LE00.IN.

176. C. A. Wolkow et al., "Regulation of C. elegans Life-Span by Insulinlike Signaling in the Nervous System," *Science* 290, no. 5489 (2000): 147–50.

177. The oldest person on record was Jeanne Louise Calment, who lived to 122.

178. Yuval Noah Harari, *Sapiens* (Toronto: McClelland & Stewart, 2014), 271.

179. Aubrey de Grey, "A Roadmap to End Aging," TED video, July 2005, https://www.ted.com/talks/aubrey_de_grey_says_we_can_avoid_aging?language=en#t-287106.

180. Zoë Corbyn, "Live for Ever," *Guardian*, Jan. 11, 2015, http://www.theguardian.com/science/2015/jan/11/-sp-live-forever-extend-life-calico-google-longevity.

181. World Health Organization, "Dementia Cases Set to Triple by 2050 but Still Largely Ignored," April 11, 2012, http://www.who.int/mediacentre/news/releases/2012/dementia_20120411/en.

182. Andrew Goldman, "Ray Kurzweil Says We're Going to Live Forever," *New York Times Magazine*, Jan. 25, 2013, http://www.nytimes.com/2013/01/27/magazine/ray-kurzweil-says-were-going-to-live-forever.html?_r=0.

183. John Hendrickson, "Can This Man and His Massive Robot Network Save America?" *Esquire*, May 19, 2015, http://www. esquire.com/news-politics/interviews/a35078/transhumanist-presidential-candidate-zoltan.

184. Adam Pez, *The Silicon Rapture* (Vancouver: Nonvella, 2015).

185. Stanislaw Ulam, "John von Neumann, 1903–1957," *Bulletin of the American Mathematical Society* 64, no. 3 (May 1958), 1–49.

186. *32 Short Films About Glenn Gould*, dir. François Girard, Samuel Goldwyn, 1993 [motion picture].

187. Henry David Thoreau, *Walden* (1854; repr., New York: Knopf, 1992), 198.

188. Anne Morrow Lindbergh, *Gift from the Sea* (New York: Pantheon Books, 2005), 36.

189. Astra Taylor, *The People's Platform* (Toronto: Random House, 2014), 18.

190. John Brockman, ed., *Is The Internet Changing the Way You Think?* (New York: Harper Perennial, 2011),184–87.

191. Eva Bianconi et al., "An Estimation of the Number of Cells in the Human Body," *Annals of Human Biology* 40, no. 6 (2013), 463–71.

192. John Brockman, ed., *Is the Internet Changing The Way You Think?* (New York: Harper Perennial, 2011), 184–87.

193. H. G. Wells, *World Brain* (London: Methuen, 1938), xiv.

194. Thoreau, *Walden*, 79.

Thanks

Until you pair solitude with good company, they're both just bells un-rung. And I became deeply aware, working on this book, that the lonely life of a writer is nothing without the many brilliant friends who make that bell ring.

This book would not exist without the encouragement of my agent extraordinaire, Anne McDermid. For cheering me on and pushing me to do my best, endless thanks to: Martha Kanya-Forstner and Melanie Tutino at Doubleday, in Canada; Peter Joseph at St. Martins, in the United States; and Nick Humphrey at Random House, in the United Kingdom. And a special hat-tip to Harry Scoble at London's National Theatre, who was an early champion of the book.

Mistakes and blind-spots were limited by expert counsel from committed specialists. Among them: Matt Atchity, Nicholas Carr, Kalina Christoff, Matt Dixon, Brandy Fedoruk, Marcus

244

Frind, Allen Lau, Amy Lobben, Constant Mews, Keith Oatley, Elias Roman, Christian Rudder, Natasha Schüll, John Searle, Bob Stein, Jeff Temple, Marius Ursache, Marshall Van Alstyne, Elizabeth Waterman, and Nora Young.

Several writers offered sage advice as I worked on this book. These include: Deborah Campbell, Douglas Coupland, Wayne Grady, and Miriam Toews.

Classroom visits were bright windows into the minds of digital natives and I'll always be grateful to the students who spoke with me at the University of British Columbia, Wilfred Laurier University, and the University of Toronto.

Like so many Canadian authors, I am deeply indebted to the Canada Council for the Arts, which provided the grant that allowed me to conduct initial research.

Then there are the friends and family who always knew when to ask about the book's progress and when to ask about the new puppy instead. The Harris and Park clans gave me more support than I deserve—especially my parents, Marilyn Harris and Bob Harris. And so many friends served as guiding lights, including David Anderson, Scott Beluz, Ed Bergman, Tyee Bridge, Anne Casselman, Trevor Corkum, Andrea Gills, Kerry Gold, April Green, Brennan Higgenbotham, Nicholas Humphries, Sean Kheraj, Dai Kojima, Michael MacLennan, Matt O'Grady, Kim Peacock, Lara Percy, Rebecca Philps, Gary

Thanks

Ross, Michael Scott, Paul Siggers, Jordan Tannahill, Pat Tu, and Elsa Wylie.

Thanks, finally, to my kind and brilliant partner, Kenny Park. Nobody else can look through my writing and so easily tell the fly shit from the pepper. And nobody else can so easily pull me away from my solitude.

M.J.H.
Vancouver, Canada

Index

Index

Index

Index